GOLF
AND ALL ITS GLORY

Acknowledgements

It is clearly impossible to name everyone from the world of golf who has given time and contributed in so many different ways to the making of *Golf And All Its Glory*. It must suffice to say that without the cooperation of so many people at the very pinnacle of the game, whether it be as player, administrator, or any other role, the project could never have been completed. To all of them, a very heartfelt thanks for the warm reception that we received wherever we went.

We also thank our friends at BBC Scotland, and Titleist and Foot-Joy World-wide for their total support and without whose involvement this project would not have been possible.

Laurence St John
Donna Geils
Bruce Critchley

October 1992

GOLF
AND ALL ITS GLORY

A MODERN LOOK AT AN ANCIENT GAME

BRUCE CRITCHLEY WITH BOB FERRIER

BBC Books

PICTURE CREDITS

BBC Books would like to thank the following for providing photographs, and for permission to reproduce copyright material. While every effort has been made to trace and acknowledge all copyright holders, we would like to apologise should there have been any errors or omissions.

Courtesy of Peter Alliss page 36; Allsport pages 31, 83 (bottom), 89 (top and bottom left), 106, 114, 138–9 and 163; Colorsport pages 41, 59, 81 and 130–1; Peter Dazeley pages 68 and 166; courtesy of the European PGA page 58; courtesy of Max Faulkner page 33; Matthew Harris page 159; Hobbs Golf Collection pages 11, 24, 26, 35, 66 (left), 83 (top), 96, 97, 134, 135 and 141; Hulton Picture Company pages 9 and 74; Lawrence N. Levy, Yours in Sport pages 125 and 142; courtesy of Sidney Matthews page 93; Bryan Morgan, Golf Photography International pages 5–6, 12, 46, 61 (bottom left), 63 (bottom), 120, 154–5 and 160; Mark Newcombe, Visions in Golf pages 15, 89 (bottom right) and 186; Tony Roberts pages 101 and 146–7; Phil Sheldon pages 18–19, 29, 53, 54, 61 (bottom right), 63 (top), 66 (right), 80, 110–11, 115, 122, 126–7, 144, 151, 169, 175, 176, 182–3 and 189; Bob Thomas, Bert Neale Collection pages 73 and 99; courtesy of the USGA pages 20 and 86.

This book is published to accompany the
television series entitled *Golf And All Its Glory*
produced by Bridge Television Productions
in association with BBC Scotland
and PGA Tour Productions
which was first broadcast in 1993

Published by BBC Books,
a division of BBC Enterprises Limited,
Woodlands, 80 Wood Lane
London W12 OTT

First Published 1993
© Bridge Television Productions Ltd 1993
ISBN 0 563 36469 6
Designed by Paul Oldman

Picture research by Linda Silverman

Set in 11/14 pt Berkeley Old Style
by Selwood Systems, Midsomer Norton

Printed and bound
in Great Britain by Butler & Tanner Ltd,
Frome and London

Colour separation by Butler & Tanner Ltd,
Frome and London

Jacket printed by Lawrence Allen Ltd,
Weston-super-Mare

CONTENTS

I NTRODUCTION

This book is of course the by-product of the television series of the same name, and the idea for that came from seeing so much competitive golf over the years and knowing there were a number of interesting stories lurking behind the scenes.

Golf is more than just a game. For over 40 million people around the globe, it is an integral part of their lives and, unlike most other sports, it can be played almost from cradle to grave. Television has been one of the most fundamental elements responsible for its growth during the last 30 years and from time to time, it is nice to look beyond the daily grind of competition, and examine the roots, the mores, the traditions and the structure of this pleasurable and pervasive pastime.

The series was specifically *not* a rewrite of the 'History of Golf'; that has been done well and often. No, it was to look at issues in the game and tell stories that have not been told before, at least not all together, and not on television. And who better to tell them than those who, either as player, administrator, creator or observer, have been at the heart of those stories as they have unfolded.

You may call it an indulgence, and it probably is; but it has been a real joy to travel to many parts of the world and talk to the greats of golf, and some of the not so famous, all with fascinating things to say and views to express. This book is their words, their stories, and together they add up to a window on the world of golf as it exists today and a look back at some of the memorable and poignant moments down the years. I hope you enjoy it.

The Old Course, home of the Royal & Ancient Golf Club of **St Andrews**.

CHAPTER ONE

IN THE
BEGINNING

The history of golf as a game or pastime has been well chronicled in what we might call modern times, that is over the past two centuries. The game is much older, but its origins have been the subject of much myth and even legend. It has been established that the Romans had a popular game known as *paganica*, played with a ball of leather casing stuffed with feathers which was struck with a bent stick. The structure of the game – whether it was played to a target of sorts, whether a team or individual game, or if it was played in any type of arena – is not known.

In the reign of the English king, Edward III (1312–77), there was an edict in 1363 proscribing *cambuca* and other leisure pursuits – it was to be the first of several such edicts – in favour of archery and shooting. *Cambuca* was a ball and stick game probably related in some way to *paganica*. When David II of Scotland died six years before Edward III, he was succeeded by his sister's son Robert, the first of the Stewarts who were to rule over Scotland for three hundred years, and who have a significant place in the history of golf.

To no one's surprise in 1991, the Chinese, who seem to have invented almost everything, claimed to have been the creators of golf in an article published by one Professor Ling. It did not impress Bobby Burnet, the historian at the Royal and Ancient Club in St Andrews, who pointed out that the professor (of physical education) had supported his claim merely by producing some line drawings which anyone could have done. It appeared that he had found some very old porcelain showing hands attached to golf clubs, and some black spots which were considered to be golf holes. Burnet said, 'Anyone could do that kind of thing on a line drawing. What Ling must do is produce photographs of the porcelain, showing these things and proving that they have not been sketched on.'

There were other royal edicts against the playing of golf, notably one by James II in Edinburgh in 1457, containing the famous phrase that 'Fute ball and Golfe by utterly cryed donne, and not to be used'. Then James III in 1471 and James IV in 1491, also took exception to these activities, among others. But by the end of the century, the golfers seemed to have won. Indeed, by 1553, Archbishop John Hamilton confirmed the rights of the townspeople of St Andrews to play golf on the links (undulating sandy land that ran along the shore which had at one time been below sea level). And in time, James V, Mary Queen of Scots, James I of England, Charles I and Charles II all played golf.

In the fourteenth century in Holland, a game known as 'kolve' was played with a ball and stick. This later added to the controversy as to who had 'invented' golf. There was substantial commercial traffic between the Low Countries and the east coast of Scotland, where golf was established at Leith, Musselburgh, St Andrews, Montrose and other places. The controversy became acrimony, but historians of the game now conclude that both pursuits probably arose in parallel and

This ice scene by Antonie Van Stroelin (pre 1699) reflects the Dutch game of 'kolve'.

are content to leave it at that. Golf in Scotland from the very beginning was played to a hole in the ground. The Dutch played to a mark – a post, a doorway or the corner of a bridge.

When the crowns of Scotland and England were united in 1603, and James I settled in London, he played golf at Blackheath, and the Royal Blackheath Club is listed as dating from 1608 although the evidence for that is slender. By 1616, the feathery ball was established in place of balls of 'turned wood or flock'. The ball in use and its development from the feathery in those early days to the gutta-percha or 'gutty' in 1848, and then to the Haskell ball in 1902 (the rubber-wound ball), a variation of which is still in use today, was to have immense significance in the future evolution of the game. Each advance in the golf ball provoked changes in the design of courses, in the economics of the game, in playing methods and techniques, and equally importantly in the rules of the game.

The rules of golf scarcely existed before the formation of the first clubs or societies in the eighteenth century, and each of these had its own individual code. The Gentlemen Golfers of Leith played over Leith Links and changed their name to the Honourable Company of Edinburgh Golfers in March 1744. They played their matches to their code, the famous '13 rules'. When the Society of St Andrews Golfers was founded ten years later, they adopted all but one of the Honourable Company rules. By the end of the century, other societies were in existence at Aberdeen, Musselburgh, Crail, even Glasgow, and exiled Scots were to form a club in Manchester in 1818. For a time, the Honourable Company lost its home at Leith and was virtually in suspension. It went to Musselburgh in 1836, sharing with the Royal Musselburgh Club (1774) and was never really settled until it went to Muirfield in 1891. The reputation of St Andrews as the guardian of the sport (the St Andrews golfers became the Royal and Ancient Golf Club of St Andrews in 1834), steadily increased. When the Prestwick Club was formed in 1851, it accepted the 'St Andrews rules'. So too did Royal Blackheath, and irony of ironies, the Honourable Company eventually accepted the 'St Andrews rules'. Yet the clubs were closely linked from the beginning. In the first decade or so after 1754, the Hon. Francis Charteris, Sir Henry Seton, Thomas Boswall and William St Clair of Roslin were all on the lists of captains of both clubs.

These early clubs were sustained by such men of property. Their pleasure was in the arranging of matches, and in dining afterwards, in a clubhouse or adjoining inn, where the golfers would keep a cellar of

fine claret. The original Gentlemen Golfers of Leith supped in Luckie Clephan's tavern at Leith. The Open Championship trophy to this day is appropriately a claret jug. Before the coming of the gutty ball, the game was for the wealthy. Going back no further than 1850, a feathery ball would cost in modern terms £120–150, against today's ball costing £2. A golf club would cost much the same as a ball then, so that at least has stayed in line with inflation.

The Cardinal Bunker at **Prestwick** (circa 1890) where the Open began.

Only gentlemen and aristocrats could afford to play on the course proper. There was probably a substantial business for small boys searching for featheries under the bushes, and trying to re-sell them. Such a ball lasted for only a few rounds in any event. Mishit badly, it could explode. There may have been another level of golf played in those days, before the advent of the gutta percha ball, by commoners, playing in and around the churchyard with a golf club cut from a hedgerow and a turned wood ball. Amusing golf can be played around headstones. The gutty ball was harder than the feathery. It flew and ran further, putted better and was much cheaper, and its arrival in 1848 changed everything. But it needed a more powerful hit and put an excessive strain on the elegant clubs of the time which were long in the shaft, with shallow faces and long swan-like necks and heads that had been used to sweep the feathery away. Now clubs had to be deeper in the face, heavier in the head and shorter from heel to toe.

Before the gutty, golf had been a running game to a large extent – putters were used from as far away as 100 yards from the hole – but now, more and more, the ball flew through the air. And more and more 'iron' clubs were forged for definite purposes, such as hacking the ball out of ruts and holes and cart tracks.

These consequences – the ball in the air and a shorter punchier swing – seem to have followed every advance in golf's equipment. A very long shot with a feathery ball would be 180 yards. The gutty passed that distance comfortably. So courses had to be lengthened, bunkers added or replaced. The cheapness of the ball and the spread of the railway system, brought an expansion in the number of golfers and the number of courses, particularly in England, but also abroad. Travelling Scots, traders, soldiers, governors and Empire builders, took the game with them. The Scottish regiment of the Black Watch was largely responsible for Lahinch (1893) that marvellous links course in the west of Ireland. Another Highland regiment, the Argyll and Sutherland Highlanders, together with the Royal Engineers, started golf in Hong Kong (1889). Sir James Fergusson, an Edinburgh man and Governor of South Australia took golf to Adelaide in 1869. But the Royal Calcutta in which Scots certainly had a hand, is the oldest golf club outside the British Isles (1829).

Royal Calcutta – the oldest golf club outside the United Kingdom.

Although golf had been invariably a match play affair, of knock-out matches between individuals, when the Open Championship was staged by the Prestwick Club initially, in 1860, it was decided at stroke play. In promoting the competition, Prestwick was supported by both the R & A and the Honourable Company. In 1870, after the original prize of a belt had been won outright by young Tom Morris for three consecutive wins, the championship was abandoned for a year, before recommencing with a new prize of a claret jug (still played for to this day) and this time rotating around Prestwick, St Andrews and Musselburgh, by then the home course of the Honourable Company. The Royal Liverpool Club was founded in 1869 with its nine-hole course on the Hoylake racecourse and in 1885 it staged an open amateur event which became the Amateur Championship. Such clubs as Prestwick, Liverpool and the Honourable Company agreed to bring a code of rules up to date in 1893 and, in 1897, all the clubs agreed to adopt the St Andrews rules and make the R & A the final authority. Thus the Rules of Golf Committee came into being.

The United States Golf Association was formed in 1894 and the game in America expanded rapidly. Similar associations were formed in all the countries of the world which had embraced the game. All the other countries had a centralized national governing body, whereas the British left that to a club in golf, as in racing with the Jockey Club and cricket with the Marylebone Cricket Club. The United States' Association accepted the St Andrews code of rules, appending certain rulings of their own. One R.H. Robertson, elected President of the USGA in 1901, was concerned that America might be 'held down by precedent and tradition', clearly meaning the R & A. He also declared that he should like to see 'American Golf'.

Over the next decade, there were many differences of opinion over the 'Schenectady' putter which had the shaft inserted into the centre of the blade, and which Walter Travis, an amateur champion on both sides of the ocean, wielded with devastating effect. The R & A Rules Committee declared that it was a 'mallet' and therefore illegal. Charles Blair Macdonald, an American who had studied at St Andrews University, created the Chicago Golf Club, and helped found the USGA and later built the marvellous National Links of America, was the peacemaker between the two bodies.

Other differences arose though. At the autumn business meeting of the R & A in 1920 one resolution said, 'On and after May 1, 1921, the weight of the ball shall not be greater than 1.62 ounces avoirdupois and the size not less than 1.62″ in diameter. The Rules of Golf Committee and the Executive Committee of the USGA will take whatever steps they think necessary to limit the powers of the ball with regard to distance should a ball of greater power be introduced.' In adopting an 'easier and pleasanter ball for the average golfer', the USGA increased the diameter to 1.68″ in 1932, keeping the ball at the same weight. This ball 'sat up' better on the more lush fairways of America. The Canadians adopted it in 1948. A uniform world code of Rules and Practices was set up in 1951 by the R & A and USGA, when the small British ball was legalized in North America. However, in 1987, the American-sized ball of 1.68″ was adopted universally, all golfers having followed the professional lead in deciding that this was the best size for the game. The R & A though remains the governing body of golf for the entire world save for the USA and Mexico.

The governance of the game, then, rests in a little town on the East Neuk of Fife, and in an even smaller town in pastoral New Jersey. Michael Bonallack, secretary of the R & A and in his playing career five times Amateur Champion, five times English Champion and selected nine times for Walker Cup teams, looks out over the Old Course from his office atop the R & A clubhouse at St Andrews and puts the club's functions into focus:

'We have quite a wide constituency to look after. The game is expanding so rapidly. In the last couple of years, we've had Hungary, Czechoslovakia and Poland joining us. Russia has formed a golf federation and Latvia has asked to join the World Amateur Golf Council. We are also the governing authority for the Rules of Amateur Status, again apart from the USA and Mexico, and every other country in the world has its own amateur status committee, although they have to follow the code laid down here. So the club has international functions. We provide the joint chairman of the World Amateur Golf Council, which runs various international team events and which has joint secretaries. I am one of them; David Fay of the USGA is the other. The Americans had more or less their own code until 1951, when it was decided this was a nonsense. The game was becoming so international that it was agreed to have one code, and the Joint Rules Committee was formed.

'The game is highly commercial now, but I think the club has coped with it very well, in some cases has led it. The Open Championship is still run by the club. It is a commercial venture in the sense that we do try to make money from it and put it back into the development of the game all over the world. We've moved with the times. We work very closely with some of the promotion companies: we work with the PGA Tour of America, with the European PGA Tour, and these are all commercial enterprises. But it is a simple fact that if you don't go with the Open as a commercial venture, it's not going to be very popular. We remain independent. We don't pay any appearance money to any player. We think with the prize money and the prestige of the championship, we can remain independent.

'Consider the Mark McCormack organization, IMG. It has been of tremendous benefit to the R & A and the Open, but by no means do they run the Open or have any control over what happens in the championship. They come to us with suggestions, perhaps for television contracts in which they have a special expertise. They know what that market is like internationally – we don't. We deal with our own contract in this country with the BBC. But they also come to us with possible merchandising ventures in other countries which are spin offs from the Open. We have our Open Championship logo registered throughout the world, and this is sold on sweaters in Japan, and in America and Australia and various countries around the world. That was IMG's idea, and it is a good one.

Michael Bonallack OBE, Secretary of the Royal & Ancient and Britain's leading post war amateur golfer.

'When I was a young player, I looked on the R & A as the authority on the rules and the organizer of championships, but since I've become secretary, I realize that in the wider field of golf they are regarded as much more. I get letters from people asking questions on practically every subject to do with golf: domestic matters in clubs, advice on what clubs or balls to use, clothes to wear. Things that have absolutely nothing to do with the R & A. But we're thought of in some way as the spiritual leaders of the game.

'We like to think that the Open Championship is number one in the world, because it's the oldest, but I wouldn't like to think we're going to compete with the others, or claim any pecking order. That isn't right. Every great player throughout the history of the game has won the Open and it's like winning Wimbledon –

if you are a great player, you want to win it. It is special. For one thing it is always played on a links course, which the other championships are not. It was on links courses that the game really began. We travel to a rota of seven championship courses, whereas the US Open and the US PGA go to many, many more than that. They have to – America is so huge with such a large population that they have to take the championships to many different cities. The US Masters, of course, stays at the same course permanently. I think these are the differences between the Open and the others.

'Two things helped the Open Championship to grow into what it is now. One was the appearance of Arnold Palmer. In three years from 1960, he finished second, first, first, which encouraged the other young American players to make the journey. The other was the appointment of Keith Mackenzie as secretary in 1967. He was a great ideas man, and marketing man. He saw where the Open was lagging behind and he went out to persuade the best foreign players to enter the championship. He reckoned that if he attracted the best players, he'd get more and more people to watch them. That in turn meant we had to have better spectator facilities, so the Open was really the first of the big championships to have grandstands and tented villages on the grand scale. These were Keith's ideas.

'The Open is a big budget operation, but a lot of our income goes back into coaching youngsters. The future of the game rests with them enjoying it, playing and continuing to play. So we give coaching grants, not only in this country. We give money to the four home golf unions, the Ladies Golf Union, the Golf Foundation and practically every union or federation on the Continent gets a grant. We just gave some money to the New Zealand Golf Foundation. The Open Championship is not just for British players. Golfers from all these countries come to play and it is right that the countries should share the revenue. In the last few years, we've handed out some £7 million, and currently we are giving out £1 million per annum. It sounds a lot, but not when you consider the cost of golf courses these days.

'I like to think we have a very capable staff here, but we get tremendous backing from our committee members. As an international club with 1800 members, practically every profession is represented, in many cases with the leaders of their professions so we can call on the finest advice; marketing, television, legal and so on, all of which is freely given.

'The game is in good health. And it is expanding so rapidly, there is no saying where it will go. There are golf courses now in China, and when you think of the population there, growth could just go on and on. The limiting factor in the developed countries is the availability of land. It's already a problem here, and I'm sure it's going to be a problem in Europe. More specifically, with regard to the Open Championship, our biggest concern is in crowd behaviour, which has changed over the years. There is certainly a younger element coming to the Open now and golf is a much more widely-based game than it used to be. Unfortunately sometimes the behaviour isn't all that you would wish it to be. We don't want to see this creeping into golf. I hate people whistling and shouting, "Come on Nick" or "Come on Sandy," at a vital time. That doesn't help a player. If they think they are encouraging the player, they are not, they're just making it damned awkward for the player, for it spoils his concentration.

'And this crowd stampede we get at the 18th hole, the final hole of the last round, is a worry. It comes from tradition, and habit over the years. If you look at the old films of Bobby Jones playing at St Andrews, the crowd ran up the 18th fairway then. That was reasonably fine when you had a total gate of say 15 000. Now at St Andrews we can get 45 000 people in one day. If you get a fair proportion of that stampeding up the fairway, and some youngsters get in front and fall down, there could be a very nasty accident. Every year we consult with the police and the local people and the authorities, and we come up with different plans. But probably at the end of the day, it comes back to the crowd itself accepting some authority in the matter. The crowd is virtually a self-limiting factor. If there are so many people coming to the Open who find they can't see, they'll simply stop coming. That is why we aim to have half of the crowd seated, so that in the case of St Andrews, we have seating for 22 000 people. That has been a great success.'

David Fay, Executive Director of the USGA, is Bonallack's counterpart operating from the association's headquarters in Far Hills,

Overleaf:
The concept of the tented village started at the Open.

David Fay, Executive
Director of the USGA.

New Jersey. He explained how it started:

'Five US clubs; Newport, Shinnecock Hills, the Country Club
(Brookline, Boston), St Andrews and the Chicago Golf Club, met
in December 1984. They had a very nice dinner. But in 1985,
they conducted three championships, the Open, the Amateur
and the Women's Amateur. The real motivating force was the
need to establish who was the Amateur Champion, what was the
Amateur Championship. Charles Blair Macdonald, one of the
most famous figures in American golf, who became an outstanding course designer, was insistent in this matter. They all
agreed they needed a central authority to lay down the conditions of the championship, select venues and name the champion. Macdonald got his wish, and became the first American
Amateur Champion in 1985.

'We hold three open championships, the Open, the Women's
Open and the Senior Open. The US Open is clearly the principal
revenue producer for the USGA. It enables us to do other things.
We can take the revenues and put them back into the game, the
amateur game and the regional and state associations, because
we are a non-profit organization, just like the R & A. We handle
our own television contract. IMG sometimes helps with foreign
TV contracts – we are not very skilled in selling TV rights in
Malaysia! The tented village is a fairly new phenomenon in the
United States, over the last ten years or so, and we work that out
with the host club. In fact almost all of the revenue is a matter
for the host club and the USGA.

'We continue to return to courses like Baltusrol and Shinnecock Hills and Oakmont and Pebble Beach. For example, we
will play the 1995 US Amateur in Newport, where we played it
in the very first year. It is interesting that the golf courses in the
sixties were the longest in US Open history – Bellerive, Con-
gressional and so on. But we still haven't broken the 7000 yards
barrier, because we put a premium on accuracy, with fast firm
greens.

'In terms of playing the game, we still have a good number of
fine players, just because we have so many, 25 million, playing
the game. On sheer numbers, we have advantages, but we've seen
in the Ryder Cup, and in the Walker Cup at Peachtree, that the
game is no longer dominated by Americans. There are a number

of reasons for this, and one of them is the large ball. I remember when I was growing up reading about people like Peter Thomson, that he couldn't play in the United States "because he plays the small ball". We don't have that issue any more and technique seems to be worldwide. You have David Leadbetter considered the top teacher at the moment, and he is an Englishman. The world is getting smaller. There is a greater exchange of information on both technique and equipment. I wouldn't be surprised if you saw in the year 2015 a Ukranian Open Champion.'

Whilst the USGA and others have input into the rules of golf, their custodianship still lies with the R & A and it is to them that people turn for advice. John Glover, the R & A Rules expert, detailed how the game is governed through the Rules of Golf:

'We have a committee of twelve, of what we describe as home members, elected for a period of four years, and then we have twelve advisory members from around the world, one in the US, one in Canada, South Africa, two Europeans, one in Japan and so on. So everybody is involved in the process. We meet officially, formally, but a great deal of this is done by circulating papers and the home town study of nitty problems. One of the fears is that one might think that golf only happens in one's own environment, but it is played in a variety of climates, on a variety of surfaces and we have to cater for all these elements and the various things that might happen around the world, from monsoons to earthquakes.

'Golf is a very serious game, but it has an amusing side to it. We have things like snakes in some parts of the world, and the word "snake" seems to conjure up things; we have a dead snake as a loose impediment, and a live one as an outside agency, one you can move, one you cannot. One incident from the middle of Africa involved a golfer addressing the ball when unknown to him, a snake slid down a tree behind him. As the player was starting his downswing, he spotted the snake and, changing the path of his swing, whacked the snake's head off. His opponent said, of course, "Good shot" but the rules question was: was it a stroke or not? We took the view that the intention of the player to strike the ball had ceased on the way down, and that not only had he not played a stroke, but that he had converted an outside agency into a loose impediment!

'From a rules point of view we regard the USGA as partners. We have an understanding that neither of us will change anything for four years. The last revision, was in January 1992.

'Inquiries to the R & A come from everywhere, everybody. We do not respond to individuals, because we feel we might end up in a holy war with the club, but inquiries do come in from golf associations and secretaries, and if it is straightforward, they get an immediate reply. To the more difficult questions, we draft an answer in the office and send it to the Rules Committee and then the deputy chairman, who is chairman of the Decisions Committee, who will approve or otherwise, and out it usually goes. After a period of time we pick out the interesting cases and send them to the United States. They do the same for us. We then put the interesting cases in the Decisions Book. Of course, there are people who say the rules are too complex, and why don't we go back to the original 13 rules. But if you study them, they applied only to matchplay, and they didn't have a good penalty system. Others say, "Well, just let's play the ball where it lies and when you touch it, lose a stroke." But then if you hit the ball under the greenkeeper's tractor and he's at lunch that's a bit unfair. Others will argue that golf is not meant to be fair. And so it goes on.

'I think the rules have to be a combination of two things; of good sense and fairness. And they have to be as precise and as clear as possible, and at the same time, rules which are acceptable – there's no point in having a set of rules which nobody likes. The rules are not imposed on anyone, but if you want to play golf, you play to the rules. We have to keep advancing with the times, to try to clarify as much as we can, and that is an exercise which is going on. We also translate the rules into something like 25 languages, and frequently we are told, "This phrase doesn't really translate too well, can you not say it another way round, that will make it easier to understand?" Also there is the concept of equity, which is the foundation stone of golf. But some countries don't have equity – you are either guilty or not. We like to think that equity is an important part of golf, and when there are occasions which the rules don't cover, equity is the saviour. The game is basically about Mr and Mrs Smith and the weekend or Wednesday afternoon player, and not exclusively for the expert. We hope the rules are designed to cater for everybody.'

CHAPTER TWO

ALONG THE YELLOW
BRICK ROAD

.

I suppose the first real golf professional was Old Tom Morris in the sense that he was contracted by a private club. When the Prestwick club was being formed in 1851, Colonel Fairlie of Coodham, a leading personality in the new club, persuaded Tom to leave St Andrews and go west, and become 'Custodian of the Links' at Prestwick, with a wage of 15 shillings per week. Among his responsibilities were to make a final, formal design of the club's 12 holes; maintain 'the green'; make and mend clubs for the members in the little workshop behind the clubhouse; teach beginners and members, and play with members as and when required. Tom spent 14 years at Prestwick, teaching Young Tom the great game, and helped to launch the Open Championship, for The Belt, in 1860. He finished second in that inaugural event, a stroke behind the first champion, Willie Park, but went on to win it four times in the next seven years. From Prestwick he returned to St Andrews and never left the place again. If Old Tom was not the first, he may well have been the finest, living to the age of 87, and into a new century. Huge crowds attended his funeral in 1908.

Alas, not all were as proud or as noble, or as responsible, as Old Tom. The first professionals were the men who played in challenge matches; money matches. They emerged from the ranks of caddies, from club-makers, even ball-makers, and the club-makers in their turn had emerged from the ranks of joiners and carpenters and cabinet-makers. They were something of an underclass when club members were prosperous people. In those early days, in the third quarter say of the nineteenth century, the words 'amateur' and 'professional', were scarcely in use. The master/servant relationship more accurately described the state of things, the professional being at the mercy of the 'master' in being engaged to partner him in foursomes. An even lower stratum of golf were the caddies. But the professionals, it is clear, were not highly placed on the social scale.

Horace Hutchinson, a flamboyant Amateur Champion in the 1880s and an aristocratic captain of the R & A in 1918, was a man to make that clear. In *The Badminton Library – Golf*, published in 1890, he wrote:

> The professional, as we are now chiefly acquainted with him, is a 'feckless' reckless creature. In the golfing season, in Scotland, he makes his money all the day and spends it all the night. His sole loves are golf and whisky. He works at odd times – job work or time work – in the shops; but he only does it when reduced to an extremity. If he were but ordinarily thrifty, he could lay by in the autumn sufficient to carry him on through the season of his discontentment, when no golf is. He can lightly earn seven and sixpence a day by playing two rounds of golf; or if he does not get an engagement, three and sixpence a day by carrying clubs. These are about the fees paid at St Andrews and Musselburgh, which are the great manufactories of the professionals who go forth to many links as greenkeepers. Many are engaged in a kind of body-service to their masters at a pound a week, which usually includes the advantage of a breakfast in their master's house, and the disadvantage of having to black his boots. In the medal weeks they pick up a little more, and an extra shilling or two comes into their pockets from bets which they make with little judgement, but which they seldom pay if they lose. They often sell with great advantage clubs to young players, who fondly imagine magical properties to dwell in the wand itself, rather than in the hands of the sorcerers who wield it. Occasionally they combine with golf-playing more general branches of industry, which they pursue in a spasmodic fashion. Thus, when we asked of one of them whether a brother professional had no other trade than that of golf, he replied, 'Oh, aye, he has that – he breaks stanes.'

In the final decade of the last century and early in this, the achievements of J.H. Taylor, Harry Vardon and James Braid in the Open Championship, at a time when the game was expanding rapidly, brought golf home more prominently to the general public. Willie Park Jr, twice an Open Champion, brought to it business acumen in the marketing of golf clubs and in designing courses. He was also, like many another Scot, keenly aware of the possibilities of the game in America, where it was expanding even more. Alex Smith from Carnoustie sailed across in 1898, closely followed by his brothers, Willie,

Opposite:
'Old Tom'.

George and Jimmy, and there were rich dollar pickings to be had for greenkeepers, course designers and teachers from Scotland in a land where social taboos were minimal. Often a Scottish accent alone would clinch a job. Yet even champions like Vardon and Taylor, at home, would be consigned to eating a sandwich lunch in the professional's shop when playing an exhibition match. Taylor, from Westward Ho! was a man of modest beginnings, but he was particularly irked by this and he became the dynamic personality and tireless

J. H. Taylor, **Harry Vardon** and **James Braid**, the 'Great Triumvirate' painted by Clement Fisher in 1913.

organizer and canvasser who helped create the Professional Golfers'
Association in 1901. Among its objectives were:

To promote interest in the game of golf.

To protect and advance its members material and trade interests.

To hold meetings and tournaments.

To institute a Benevolent Fund.

To act as an employment agency.

Taylor's influence helped the *News of the World* newspaper, cele-
brating its fiftieth anniversary, to sponsor the PGA Match Play Championship, which it did continuously for 66 years, surely a record. The
prize money was £200 at a time when few professionals were paid £1
per week, club subscriptions were around £3, and when a first class
wooden club was less than £1. James Braid won the first event.

When Jack White, the first professional at Sunningdale and an
outstanding clubmaker, was appointed when the club opened in 1901,
he was granted 'remuneration not to exceed £1 per week, and a cottage
on the links' (this from the minute books of the club, beautifully pre-
served and leather-bound). When he won the Open Championship
three years later, the committee was so elated it voted that 'the cottage
be joined to the mains water supply'. So it was with the professionals,
as the world entered a new century. In simple terms, there was still no
question of a professional, the club servant, entering the clubouse – a
tradition which still lingers somewhat to this very day.

In America, as ever, things were slightly more advanced. The US
PGA was formed in 1916, and with World War One safely over, the US
Open Championship of 1920, staged at the Inverness Club at Toledo,
Ohio, was to become a watershed in these matters. It was the first
Open Championship on either side of the ocean at which the clubhouse was thrown open to all the players. The members of Inverness
simply decided that the professionals were their guests and should be
treated as such. It marked the beginning of the end of many social
barriers for professionals at US clubs. And the players at Inverness,
led inevitably by the ebullient Walter Hagen, put their hands in their
pockets and subscribed for an engraved grandfather clock which was
presented to the club and which stands in the foyer to this day.

This was an intriguing championship for other reasons. It
marked the last appearance in the US Open of the two famous Jersey
golfers, Harry Vardon and Ted Ray (he won the championship), and

the first appearances of such luminaries as Bobby Jones, Gene Sarazen and Tommy Armour.

In the Open Championship of the same year Hagen, making his first essay across the ocean, had rather less success at Deal.

Walter Hagen was larger than life. And very early in life, he learned that exhibition golf, tournament golf, championship golf, was show business, and whenever he appeared in public, Walter put on a show. He would arrive at the golf club and say 'Hi fellas, whose gonna be second?' He would buy champagne for the house. He made no attempt to stop the nonsense that was written about his money and his earnings, rather like the present-day speculation about Greg Norman's income, because Hagen knew that people are always fascinated by other people's income. He always had a word for the press. The other impression that was put about was of Hagen the roisterer, the party-goer, the all-night man, the big drinker. Not true. Gene Sarazen, who was close to Hagen all through the twenties, said, 'I never did see Walter drunk. He never refused a drink, but he certainly never consumed all of them.'

There are endless stories of him setting up a lunch table outside the clubhouse at Deal, and being served from the back of a limousine by his butler/chauffeur, but I am sure they are all exaggerated. He later wrote that he and Jim Barnes had entered the clubhouse on an early practice day, with no one around, when the locker room man told them they'd have to change in the pro shop. Hagen took one look at the pro shop and decided he'd do his changing in the local pub, and change his shoes in his car, which he parked every day, rather ostentatiously, in front of the clubhouse.

The world would know that, while the other professionals were changing in the back of the pro shop, Walter Hagen was not. Henry Cotton was to do much of the same in the thirties, although Henry probably had no great motivation to fight for the rights of his fellow man. As Peter Alliss says:

'I think he introduced a new way of golf. He practised for a start. He was affiliated to a club, but he had umpteen assistants. He did give some lessons, but he only gave them to the hierarchy and the people at the very top end of the social strata. Walter Hagen was flamboyant. Cotton married well. He married a woman who reportedly was enormously wealthy and so he didn't have to work but did. He was very conscious of becoming the best and he was the best.'

Gene Sarazen, the 'Squire of Germantown', was contemporary to all of this. A man of many achievements – he passed his 90th birthday in February 1992! He won the US Open in 1922 and 1932, and the Open Championship at Princes in 1932. He became one of the few players to have won both of these great championships in the same year and was the first player to put together the modern 'Grand Slam' of victories in the four major events of the US Masters, the US Open, the Open Championship and the US PGA Championship. Perhaps his greatest single moment came with the famous 'double eagle' or albatross he scored in the 1935 Masters, when he holed a 4-wood shot for a two on the par five 15th hole at Augusta, allowing him to tie and win a play-off against Craig Wood. He recalled those times:

'Well, in the early days, when I won the US Open in 1922, we were mostly considered ex-caddies! For instance, we weren't recognized in England or Scotland until we went over there and won about ten out of eleven British Open championships. And then American players were recognized throughout the world. Hagen came in there, he was Open Champion, and Bobby Jones. There were a lot of great players and they were recognized. You don't see ex-caddies winning any more – too many caddie carts! The galleries were very different in those days, just very rich people who would come to see you play, not the rank and file.

Gene Sarazen, one of only four to have won the four titles that make up the modern Grand Slam.

'In the early days of course, the pros were not allowed in the clubhouse, but I'll never forget playing with Walter Hagen, and the Prince of Wales and one of his friends, Duke so and so. At the ninth hole the prince asked us if we'd like to have a little libation. We said sure, and walked into the clubhouse and sat down, and of course all the waiters had tails on and one came over and started whispering to the Prince of Wales, and the Prince busted out, "You ought to stop this nonsense or I'll take the royal out of Royal St George's." From then on, the doors were open. But I must say, the fellows were not as fine characters as they are today. These boys are all college bred. They're more courteous to everybody. In the old days, they were all fighting each other. You always came out with a story denouncing this guy or that guy, and then he wouldn't look at you for years. It was a cut throat proposition.

'I never forget in 1922 when I won the US Open. I had my first pro job at a course in Pittsburgh and W.C. Fownes, the boss of Oakmont and president of the USGA, invited me to play

Oakmont one day since my new course was not ready. I played with him and my friend Emil Loeffler, the pro at Oakmont, and Mr Fownes said to Loeffler, "Emil this kid might have a chance to win the Open, better take him to Skokie and have a practice round." He paid all the expenses, and we went to Chicago and Skokie. And the pro there, a Scotch pro called Phil Gordon said we couldn't play the course. Emil told him that Mr Fownes had sent him, but he said it was Sunday, and we couldn't play. Emil called Mr Fownes, who told him to stand by the phone. Within half an hour we were playing. Fownes had called somebody. A month later, I was the US Open Champion, and Gordon was all smiles and couldn't be nicer to me.

'Everything was much cheaper in those days. We had an automobile, but gasoline was about 12 cents a gallon. The first prize in the British Open was $500. In the US Open and the Masters it was $500, so there was no money in it. Now they get $150 000. . . . Wheeh! I never would have won that tournament in England if it wasn't for my wife, because then we were all broke. The depression was at its height in 1932. I had no money, but she had saved some and she bought tickets to go to England, for I was ready for it. I had invented the sand iron,* which was my weakest shot. When I perfected that sand iron, I knew I had them.'

A generation later after Sarazen came another giant of the game, Byron Nelson, born in 1912. In 1945, Nelson won 18 of the 31 tournaments he entered. He averaged 68.33 per tournament round. It was probably the most extraordinary achievement by any golfer since the Bobby Jones Grand Slam. He recalled:

'The image of the golf professional was not very good at that time. The professionals were not allowed to go into the club except where the help went. Even when I was in the Ryder Cup team when we played in Great Britain in 1937, our wives were not allowed into the clubhouse. But the popularity of the game grew so much and so many people were involved in it, and the pros started growing in stature, and conducting themselves better, working hard at the job and not drinking so much that our stature grew and has grown steadily. The early pro was considered to be a servant. He was not asked into anyone's home for meals or parties or such. I don't mean he was treated badly, but he was not accepted at all from a social standpoint.

*In Sarazen's day, all iron clubs had blades of roughly the same thickness, and for bunker shots these had a tendency to dig into the sand. Sarazen, during one of his early plane flights, noted the lift effect caused by movement of the flaps. He applied the same principle to his golf club, which resulted in the broad flange on the bottom of the modern sand iron, with the back of the flange below the leading edge of the face.

'It probably started to get better with the championship at Inverness, in Toledo, a wonderful club, when the pros were allowed in and made welcome. The media people were happy about it. They were allowed in, too, for the first time. So it all grooved together gradually, it didn't happen overnight. Most of the pros on the tour today have gone through college and universities. At that time they had not. They were uneducated because it wasn't a job that needed that kind of atmosphere. I became a professional rather by accident. I had become a pretty good amateur in the state of Texas, and won a lot of golf tournaments. I had won the All Southwest Championship, then another tournament in Oklahoma, which became the Trans-Mississippi in 1931, an important tournament.

'I became a professional at Texarkana CC where they had a professional tournament with a prize of $500. They had a good field of people who became name players later. I needed money. I didn't have any, didn't have a job – jobs were scarce in the early thirties. I went over, handed in $5 entry, played in the tournament, finished third and made $75. It was the most money I had ever seen in my life.

Byron Nelson – will his record of 11 consecutive tournament victories ever be equalled.

'I had a club job all of my life, until I left the tour in 1946. I was never able to make a living from playing tournaments, even when winning. I won 54 tournaments and five major championships, but I averaged only $14 000 a year. In a way, that was a lot of money, but there were caddie fees, hotels, food, laundry, cleaning, travel. It was necessary. There just wasn't that much money to be played for in the tournaments. You worked hard at the club, selling to the members. You didn't have all these stores selling golf goods in town then. On the tour, there were few motels. You stayed in hotels, or in bed and breakfast places. Hotels would sometimes give us a special rate. You travelled by car almost entirely. Then along came the DC-3, a great old plane which made aviation what it is. You had no pressurized cabin. You were allowed 40 lbs of luggage. My luggage and my wife's luggage weighed over 40 lbs, the golf bag stuffed with clubs, balls and shoes weighed 40 lbs so you had to buy an extra ticket – they took only so much weight. And if it had more than that, you'd have to buy another ticket. So it was expensive. The tour was arranged so that one town followed another, and mostly we drove.

'Travel was one of the problems for us playing in Britain. I went over in 1937 with the Ryder Cup team. I was fortunate to be on that team, it was the first time the USA had won over there. I played in the Open and finished fourth. Henry Cotton won it. The thing of it was, I was a poor sailor. I didn't like the water, and don't today. You had to ride a boat then, and it took four days to get over. Then you played and then you got on the boat and went back. It was always in the middle of the summer, so you blocked out a whole month. I won $187 from the Open, so I said no more of that. Arnold Palmer gave it stature of course, but the thing that really did it was aviation. You could fly over there, fly back and play in a week. Lee Trevino won the Canadian Open, the American Open and the British Open in a total of 19 days – impossible in my time.

'But I must say I am very pleased that they make the money they do today. The money they make is not to be compared like the other athletes in baseball or football or basketball, where they can have a poor year and still make money. The pros who play on the tour get no guarantees.'

Max Faulkner, Open Champion of 1951, was one of the great

characters of his day. When he was an assistant to Henry Cotton at Royal Mid-Surrey in the late forties, he had his fun, but his tales underline the lingering attitudes that golf professionals had to endure:

'Oh dear, oh dear, you'd laugh. Oliver Wynn and Jack Knipe were Henry's leading assistants, number one and number two. The pro shop at Mid-Surrey had a toilet, but it was a bit difficult and awkward to get in – Henry had lots of clubs in there. So one day, Oliver and Jack walked right in through the main door of the club, went straight to the gents, did the business, washed their hands and came out again. I was in the shop when there came a helluva bang on the hatch. "What's this?" I said. There was the secretary, a bad-tempered sort of fellow, drank a bit at night. He handed me an envelope and said, "Give that to your number one assistant, or to Henry Cotton." Jack Knipe got hold of it, opened it, and it read, "Under no circumstances shall Henry Cotton's staff enter the clubhouse forthwith. Signed. The Sec." So we weren't allowed to go near the front of that clubhouse.'

Max was told, when he first went to Mid-Surrey, that he could have a shower in the clubhouse once a week, at 8.15 on Monday mornings! And even after the war, some thirty years since the then Prince

Max Faulkner, one of the great characters of post War British golf.

of Wales' patronage of golf had done so much for the American professional, the old British class system still ruled; as Faulkner shows:

> 'The Open was at Royal St George's in 1949, and I went down there the week before, I'll never forget it. I had my clubs on my shoulder, walked in the door, and a few steps down a passageway someone walked towards me and said, "Who are you, what do you want?" I said, "I'm Max Faulkner. Would you mind if I played here for a week's practice sir, I want to win the Open?" "You're not allowed in here," he said. "Go over to the pro shop and he'll let you change your clothes in his workshop. No professionals are allowed in here." I thought, "Good God." You know I was a pretty good player, in those days. I played in the 1947 Ryder Cup, but I was tossed out.'

In his time with Cotton, Faulkner would go with him each winter to Monte Carlo, where Henry had a golf school, charging his clients large amounts of money to hit balls into the sea. Cotton had been a professional on the Continent, in Brussels, before the war and was infatuated with Europe and the European way all his life. He had good reason. There, the game was higher up the social scale than in Britain. There were comparatively few clubs, and all of them were centres of major social activity. Britain was seen as the important golfing nation, and having British professionals was *de rigeur* for these clubs. With things as they were in the twenties and thirties, the cream of British pros found the financial rewards and the social status there much more inviting than at home.

Henry Cotton has a powerful claim to be considered the finest modern British player, Jacklin, Faldo, Lyle and Woosnam notwithstanding. Along with Faldo he is the only player to have won the Open three times since the great and somewhat different days of Vardon, Braid and Taylor. He was immensely successful and he was different from all his contemporaries in one significant fact – he was certainly not an ex-caddie. He did not come from a poor background. Henry was the son of a prosperous foundry owner who was later in the garage business. He went to a good public school, and before he left, he had resolved to become not a golfer but a champion golfer. He found a job at the Fulwell club as a junior assistant, sandpapering iron heads and shaving hickory shafts. He then moved to Rye, and at the age of only 19, became the top pro at Langley Park. Cotton made himself a great

Henry Cotton after receiving the Open trophy at Carnoustie in 1937.

player simply by practising, endless practising, and by thinking about it. He thought about everything – diet, sleep, his physical condition, lifestyle, equipment – and he was a smarter, more selfish thinker than all the others.

Cotton is generally considered to have led the British pros out of bondage, out of the wilderness of the back shop into the sunlight of the clubhouse and proper treatment, but I suspect it was less dramatic than that, and not a considered, deliberate policy on his part. When Henry changed in the clubhouse car park, à la Walter Hagen, it was for his convenience, not for any crusade. As Max Faulkner said, 'He had a way about him, he wasn't having any nonsense from anyone. We looked up to him, the first one to put our game at a higher level. He stayed in hotels, the better hotels. We followed him. He took us out of bed and breakfast, and into hotels when we could afford them.'

He went, first class on the *Aquitania*, to America when he was 21, and made a long trip to Argentina. He won the Belgian and Czech Opens. A fluent French speaker, he was the man for the good life. Invited to be professional at Ashridge to get the club moving, on his return from Brussels, he told them he would require honorary membership, and a covered practice area for winter teaching. He dressed impeccably, driven along by Toots, his wife who had pursued his sleek, dark, aristocratic good looks all the way from Argentina. For years he lived in a suite at the Dorchester Hotel, then in a town house in Eaton Square in London's Belgravia. When he had retired from play, he designed a course on a rice paddy at Penina in Portugal's Algarve, and became the professional, spending his closing years there. From the early thirties through most of his life, Henry Cotton was a spectacular figure in British and international golf. And he pulled his peers along, and up with him, by example.

Other British players followed Cotton's example, if to a lesser degree. Arthur Lees, who was for many years at Sunningdale, spent some time in Czechoslovakia. Percy Alliss went to Berlin to the Wannsee Club. His son, Peter, reckons that from 1926 when he went there, until 1932, when he left because of the rising menace of Hitler, he probably earned no less than £4000 a year – a very substantial reward indeed in the twenties.

Peter Alliss's dad, Percy. Like father, like son, Ryder Cup players.

Peter says,

'Strange. My father served in the Argyle and Sutherland Highlanders in the First World War, and had been shot twice by the

Germans, and there he was. At Wannsee he was the professor, highly respected, very important, treated on a level plane. Rather like the old Scottish golf professionals going to America at the turn of the century and breaking into new ground which they did, he went to Germany. Henry Cotton followed and went to France and Belgium. Audrey Boomer also. Because there was something about being a golf professional on the Continent that wasn't available in Britain. You were just a glorified caddie in many people's eyes and very much the sort of lower figure. Whereas there you actually went as if you had a university degree and you were the master and they were the pupils and they were prepared to pay for it.

'When we came back to England, and eventually settled at the Ferndown Club, it was very much surname stuff. It was Alliss the pro. A few of the younger fellows called him Percy or Mr Alliss, but it was very much that he was the servant.

'And I don't see anything much wrong with that. Today's society tries to eliminate surnames and it's all buddy, buddy stuff. And I find it always very difficult to give anyone the sack when it's been all buddy buddy stuff and we come round to your house for drinks and you come to mine. And you call my wife Ethel, although her name happens to be Jackie, and that's probably why you got the sack. I don't think you can have this sort of relationship and call somebody into the office and say clear your desk. That's just my old-fashioned view of the way things are. My father was well respected, a man of humour, gentle humour, but he wouldn't be sat upon.'

What with the war it was perhaps two generations before Peter moved into the professional world, but things hadn't really changed.

'I turned pro when I was 15, yet my father, with all his knowledge of golf and the golf trade and all its personalities, could get me only one deal – a set of clubs at $10\frac{1}{2}$ per cent discount. Our Ryder Cup team in 1947 had been very badly beaten in America, and there was much talk in 1949 of "giving new lads a chance". Leonard Crawley and Henry Longhurst, great golf writers of the time, said what about young Alliss. It was mentioned at Ferndown, my father's club, and mine come to that, that I would be the youngest player to play for Britain, and wouldn't it be a nice thing if I was allowed into the clubhouse! They had a committee meeting about it, and they decided to wait to see if I was selected for the Ryder Cup team as to whether I would be worthy of being allowed into the clubhouse. So I went through a period where you got honours by doing something or paying your dues or whatever way you want to put it. Knowing your place. And I must confess, I don't think that's all together a bad thing. I think a lot of today's problems are caused by people who have talent who have access to dollars, yens, pounds, cents, and they take it as their birthright to barge in wherever they want to go because of the "don't you know who I think I am" syndrome. And I find it a bit of a pain in the neck.'

Max Faulkner, too, was a professional in his teens, and says, 'Before the war, it was a bit of a scrounge. My father, Gus, was a pro, at one time seventh assistant to James Braid if you please. He put me to making golf clubs, filing down shafts, great thick hickory shafts. It gave me good hands, very strong fingers.'

Max Faulkner was beginning to make an impression on the game, winning regional events, when the war came – 'I put my clubs in the attic and joined the RAF.' He was 23, only just out of the service, in 1946, when he won the Dunlop Tournament at Southport –

'Four hundred and fifty quid, I thought my God, I'm a millionaire. I never looked back. I was really a tournament player, I played in everything I could. At Mid-Surrey, Henry didn't pay me anything – I got around £1 a round for playing with a member and played almost every day. It gave me a base. And Henry said I had a flair for teaching. Ten shillings an hour I charged, eight hours a day if I could get it. I got along very well with Henry.

'I won lots of tournaments, Dunlop, Penfold, Lotus, the Spanish Open, the Portuguese Open. When I went to Portrush for the the 1951 Open, I knew I would win before I went, for some reason. In 1949 and 1950, I had finished fifth and sixth, and got the taste for it. I had a putter, 11 ounces, that I couldn't miss with, couldn't miss the hole. I thought, "Hey, I've got to win this, I'm bound to win this." I was 71 first round, three shots behind. I did 70 the second round, a bit of wind about. That got me two ahead. No ropes on the course then. I used to have to ask people would they mind moving back a bit. You could see the colour of everybody's eyes, they were so near. I had 70 in the third round and was six ahead. I had two great plates of steak and kidney pie and, walking to the tee for the afternoon round, a man said, "Would you mind signing that golf ball for my son, he's about 12." I did, and he said, "Put 1951 Open Champion will you – you're bound to win!"

'I said, "Oh, hold on guvnor." Then I thought, "Well I'm bound to." So I wrote it. I still have nightmares when I think of that. When I won the Open, I had on my yellow shoes and canary trousers. The canary shoes were knocked off twice with people rushing by. My caddie swore and cursed because they were hitting his bag. I'd bend down and the spectators, rushing you see, knocked me over and I'm trying to put my shoe on. That happened twice the last day of the Open.'

Max Faulkner was at his prime in the fifties. His career reached back to the last of the hickory shafts. In his time he seldom played more than a dozen events each year at a time when the tour in America was expanding speedily. That meagre schedule of work kept many fine amateurs from turning professional. Joseph Carr of Dublin dominated the amateur scene in the fifties, winning the Amateur Championship three times. In his long career, he won a hamperful of Irish national titles and was a Walker Cup man ten times. Asked why he didn't turn professional, Joe said, 'No money in it, Bruce, no money in it at all. And at that time you had to wait five years as some kind of apprentice before you could take prize money. Perhaps if I had been younger I might have done it, but I can't think I would have changed my life, I've lived it and loved it and wouldn't change it.'

As Joe Carr dominated the fifties, so Michael Bonallack was the outstanding amateur golfer of the sixties. He agreed with Carr:

'When I was young enough, I wasn't good enough. When I was good enough, I wasn't young enough. You don't want to start turning pro when you are in your mid-thirties and go chasing around the world, especially if you have a young family as I had. If there had been more money in it, I might have been tempted. I'm not sure I would have enjoyed it, or have been successful at it, because I found it very difficult to gear myself up for more than two or three big events in a year. I had a limited amount of holiday time, so I would plan my events and concentrate on these. So I'm not sure I'd have enjoyed it, or even been able to do it every day as the pros have to. In my time, you had quite a lot of spectators, quite a lot of Press, at the Amateur Championship.

But amateur golf has lost its audience because professional golf has grown tremendously and its standards have grown too. For any amateur considering a professional career, he should first prove to himself that he can win major amateur events, as people like Nick Faldo and Sandy Lyle and Steve Richardson have done.'

All this, then, was the background to the golfing world which Tony Jacklin entered. His career was to have a profound effect on British professional golf and the British and European tournament scene. Tony Jacklin was born in Scunthorpe in July 1944. He was to win the Open Championship at the age of 25 in 1969, and the US Open within a year. The material rewards were immense by the standards of the time – the instant Rolls Royce, and a succession of impressive residences in the West Country of England, the island of Jersey and the Costa del Sol in Spain. As he approached the age of fifty, he was installed in a country manor in southern Scotland, concentrating on golf course design and construction, and reminiscing:

'The kind of life I grew up in was very different to the kind of life I am leading now. My father drove a locomotive in the local steel works in Scunthorpe, in Lincolnshire.

'He took me to golf when I was about eight years old, and I went with him to the local course, and played around. Within a year I was besotted with the game, happiest when I was out on the golf course. That's where I dreamed my dreams. I didn't have the benefit of good tuition when I was young, so to a large degree I was self taught. It was trial and error, copying good players, and by the time I was 13 years old, I had a 12 handicap, pretty good in that part of the world. One of the most significant things about my early life in golf was that in my area it was not a particularly popular game. When I was 13, I won the Lincolnshire Junior Championship. There were eight entrants, in spite of the fact that Lincolnshire was the second biggest county in England then. Now there would be forty, I'm sure. When I was 15, I played for England Boys against Scotland, at Dalmahoy near Edinburgh, in 1959 I think. Then at 16, I won the Lincolnshire Open Championship. That was against the professionals.

'That was precisely when I decided that I wanted to turn pro. We didn't have the funds for that, so I did what about 70 per cent of the population of Scunthorpe seemed to do, I went to work at the steel works. Had a year there as an apprentice fitter, didn't

Tony Jacklin on his way
to winning the 1969
Open Championship.

enjoy it, but still played a lot of golf. I applied for a job at Potter's
Bar, north London, where Bill Shankland was professional, and
I was successful in getting an interview. At that point, I told my
dad what I had done, and asked him if he would take me down
to the interview, and said that if he didn't think professional golf
was a good idea after we had made that trip, why, I wouldn't do
it. He agreed, so off we went in November 1961.

'Bill Shankland was a larger than life figure, a great salesman,
and he certainly convinced my dad that this was the life for a
young fellow, so I started there, in January 1962. I remember
when I arrived there the snow was three feet deep. We had a terrible winter that year, and Mr Shankland said, "You'd better go
home, we can't do anything here." I said I couldn't go home, that
this was it for me, this was it. So I spent the first three months in
the shop, doing any repairs that needed to be done and I soon
found out that I didn't like that side of it, but I had learned much
of that through the professional at the Scunthorpe Golf Club, so
I made it my business to practise harder and keep on at it,
because I wanted to play tournament golf.

'The tournament players were the stars of the game, and in the early sixties probably more so if they were foreign. The British attitude to their pros had been slightly down the nose. But for example, Harold Henning from South Africa was a friend of one of the members and he would come and play and people really did tend to look up to that kind of individual. The Gary Players, the Arnold Palmers, Jack Nicklauses, they were the gods. The home-bred pros were less likely to get that respect and attention from certain British club members. Mr Shankland might go into the clubhouse, but only on certain occasions. He didn't abuse the privilege. Assistants, unless they were invited, didn't – I can't remember having been in there at all during my first year there, other than in the winter when the course was closed and under supervision we would go in for a game of snooker.

'I started my career, as it were, about 1964 with the help and backing of some members of the club. They worked out a wonderful system for me. They didn't give me money, but they indicated that if I didn't cover my expenses, they would help me out with them. So they saved me the embarrassment of having to ask for a loan, and allowed me a certain feeling of security in the whole thing. I was a pretty determined and maybe proud young fellow and didn't really want to go asking for money if I could help it. And more often than not, I got by. We are talking now, of course of first prizes of around £750 in British professional tournaments at this time.

'The president of the club was a man called John Rubens, now deceased. I had some close friends there, still have. Another was Wally Dubabney with whom I used to play a lot of golf. My first crack at the Open was in 1963, at Lytham St Annes, when I finished thirtieth. Although I had won some money, they didn't give it to me – the procedure is that they post it on. Wally gave me a fiver, to get home. It must have been for train fare. I don't believe I had a car then! And when I made my first overseas trip, John Rubens organized the money side of it. He asked me what I had planned. I told him I hoped Dunlop would put in £200. I had saved £200, and he said that if he put in £200, that would do it. Off I went, spent the money, and won £35. The experience was good, the next year 1965 I won more than I spent.

'Prior to my second trip, I went to John to give him his £200 back. He asked what I was doing this time and I said the same thing. He said if he gave me £100, he would have put up half of the trip. I said yes but ... He said, "Go on, go on." I won the last tournament I played and won £1000. And when I went to give him his money back, he said, "Oh, buy something for your wife." He was that kind of man.

'One of the greatest pleasures I got out of winning my first tournament in America was that he was there. I played my final round with Arnold Palmer and Don January, and there was Johnny Rubens, inside the ropes, walking along with us. He happened to be in Jacksonville on business, he said. But the fact that the man who had done most for me in those early days was there to see my first victory was thrilling to me.

'It would have been impossible for me to win or sustain the kind of pressure I was under in winning the British Open, if I hadn't gone to America when I did, and learned how to cope with the pressure over there. Because there was no question then, the American tour was far and away the biggest and best tour in the world and you weren't considered a player until you could win on the US tour.

'What I tried always to do, and I believe I succeeded, was to move on and up. As soon as I was comfortable at one level of the game, I wanted to move on. I became a county golfer, then county champion. In my first year as a pro I won the Middlesex Assistants. The next year, 1964, I won both the Coombe Hill and Gor-ray Assistants Championship, nationals. And in 1965, I won my first full professional event, the Blaxnit Tournament in Belfast. It was to be the tournament life for me. Bill Shankland's shop and dusting and mending, were fading fast.'

It is impossible to exaggerate the enormity of Jacklin's achievement in the late '60s and early '70s. Palmer and Nicklaus were rampant on the world stage, the latest and possibly greatest, of more than half a century of American golfing giants. Since Cotton, no Briton had come remotely close to challenging their domination of the game. And with all the stars that have emerged in Europe these last few years, still no European has matched Jacklin's achievement in winning the US Open Championship.

For a variety of reasons, Jacklin's spell at the top was not as long as it might have been. Being the sole British star, every time he teed the ball up, the media attention and public expectation was enormous. That inevitably took its toll. However, in 1972, he had a great chance to win the (British) Open again, this time at Muirfield.

Towards the end of the third round, and in the last group with Lee Trevino, he was a handful of shots ahead of the field. Trevino takes up the story:

'In that third round, I was way behind Jacklin. I birdied 14 with a 20 footer, 15 with a 15 footer. Knocked it into the hole on the fly from a bunker at 16. Birdied 17, Then chipped in from the back of 18. I birdied the last five holes, nobody has ever said anything about that. The next day, Nicklaus was six shots back, but he'd caught us on number nine. He eagled number nine and caught us. We were dead even, Jacklin and I and Nicklaus. But Jacklin and I also eagled nine, the par five, and we went ahead of Jack. The mistake Jack made was he bogeyed 16 and I thought Jacklin was going to win the tournament. I had given up on 17, that last day – drove it into the bunker, had to go out sideways and hit a 2-wood short of the green. I wasn't on the green in three. Jacklin had a 20-footer for birdie. I chipped my ball up so I could try to make par, and chipped it clear over the green. I walked over there and was so mad that I didn't have time to cool off, because my caddie beat me to the ball. Now if Willie Aitchison had waited and I would have gotten over, I'd have cooled off a little bit, but the bag was sitting there, I took out a 9-iron. chipped it down, and the ball went in the hole.

'I didn't even get a good grip, hardly set my feet. It was a give up, because I had already told Jacklin, "Take it on out, baby." I said, "take it on out, I'm cooked. You can stick a fork in me, I'm done." And he three putted. I made him so nervous by chipping in, he three putts it. Then I knock it about five feet from the hole on 18 with an 8-iron and I remember Nicklaus telling me, as soon as he saw me swing that 8-iron, on television, he never watched any more. He knew the ball had to be close to the hole.

'Jack ended up beating Tony out of second place. He quit after that, he quit. I mean I thought Tony Jacklin was one of the best players I had ever seen. When he won at Hazeltine in the US Open of 1970, by seven or eight shots, that was unbelievable how he took that golf course apart. Great ball striker, good putter, very well rounded game, but something clicked when I chipped in all these times to beat him out of a British Open. He couldn't take it any more, couldn't stand it, just absolutely quit. It's too bad. Golf lost a great competitor, I thought, a great golfer. But that's the way it is in the majors – when your chilli is hot, that's the whole feeling. It's like a gambler instinct. When you're hot, you keep going.'

Tony Jacklin was inclined to agree.

'In the seventies, I was capable from tee to green, but I suffered in the Open of '72, when Lee chipped in. I was motivated tremendously, self-motivated, my greatest attribute was my self-confidence. That was pretty much dented in '72 when Lee did what he did. It knocked the wind out of my sails to a degree. I was never really the same after that. I'm not blaming Lee, it was just the circumstances. I spent all my professional playing life trying to win those majors again. I have no regrets. I don't look back in anger. I did what I did, won what I won. Many great players have played this game and not won a single major.'

Jacklin played on for 10 more years, ending his career with a win in the 1982 PGA Championship. But his contribution to Europe's golfing folklore didn't end when he stopped competing. In due course, he inherited the mantle of Ryder Cup captaincy and brought to that task the same single-minded pusuit of success that so characterised his own playing career. No one will deny that he was the first British or European captain to have the raw material to do the job, but the secret was to build a team to overturn the sheer weight of history.

From his own playing days he remembered the awe in which the Americans were held. Better dressed, glamorous wives and always travelling first class, they seemed to start two up before a ball had even been struck. From the moment he became Captain, he demanded the same for his team. His first match was over there and they flew in on Concord, and only failed by a whisker to be the first to win on American soil. That moment was only delayed till he led his team back there four years later, and by then they travelled as holders of the Ryder Cup and as favourites to retain it.

Because of Lee Trevino's efforts at Muirfield and the pressures imposed by public and media attention to every shot he hit, not to mention his total immersion in the Ryder Cup during the 1980s, Jacklin had ceased to compete by the time he was 40. Had he known

Tony Jacklin in his capacity as Captain for the fourth time, with the **Ryder Cup team of 1989**.

then (1984), just how big the US Seniors Tour was to become by the time he hit 50, and just how much money there would be to win there, he might have kept his game and competitive spirit in racing trim for another shot at the big time. And he still might. Trevino couldn't wait, and gave up an almost unbelievably lucrative commentating contract to return to competitive golf full time.

'I get everything in perspective. I practised for five and a half months for the Senior Tour. I knew it was coming. I did it every day, every single day. It was like when I was defending champion at the 1972 British Open at Muirfield. That was the only time I practised for a major championship. I never practise for a major championship. I go right from the other tournament to play in a major championship. If there is something wrong with your game when you get there, you ain't gonna find it there. It's the old deal, "You gotta dance with who brung you". If I play well, I play well. That particular championship, we were taking five other couples as well as my wife and I. We were staying at Gifford, near Muirfield. Now Jack Nicklaus had won the Open and the Masters in 1972, and he was going for the third one, the third leg of the majors. It happened that Orville Moody was about to open a new club in Coline, Texas, opening on the Sunday I was leaving. So I went there in advance, practised, dawn 'til dark, ran five miles a day. Must have hit a thousand balls a day to go defend my title. And I did it. I defended it. I won it. It was the same in preparing for that first year on the senior tour.'

Before he moved up to senior level, Trevino quipped that he was tired of playing with 'the flat bellies – I want to play with the round bellies'. Arnold Palmer spoke of how it was with the round bellies:

'First of all, I had more or less laid out my life with the thought that at a certain age, my world globetrotting and my golfing prowess would be slowed greatly, and that would be by age. When I saw the Senior Tour coming on I had to make some alterations to the schedule I had laid out for my life. Some I couldn't make. But the Senior Tour – I think we all felt that it might be successful. I don't think any of us ever imagined that it could become full-time golf, professionally, as it has become. We anticipated a growing situation, but not one that within ten years would become a $20 million enterprise that would bring people out of retirement, people who had thought they would never again come out and play golf in public. And making some heroes of people who even if they had played golf all their lives, never did quite make it. Now they are acknowledged as great players on the Senior Tour and I think that's great.

'I think it has caught the attention of not just senior citizens but also young people. And I think it has given the regular tour players something who, when they reach 40 are thinking generally, or did, "What am I going to do with the rest of my life?" All of a sudden now people who are 40 are looking forward to being 50 so that they can become senior players. I've heard that so often. It is quite amazing when you hear people say, "God I wish I was 50, I'd be out there playing on the Senior Tour." It has given these people an opportunity to continue with the same life style and the same things they have enjoyed for so many years. One of the reasons for its success is that the names are household names, whether it be Sam Snead, Julius Boros, Jack Nicklaus, Lee Trevino or Gary Player. These names are very important, very recognizable and they have a niche in the game of golf that people understand and recognize. The other thing is its value in consumer dialogue – from industry – from the advertiser to the public, whether it be Cadillac automobiles or GTE or telephones. We have found something that gets to the customer, the consumer. And the consumer may well be the purchaser of the Cadillac, someone of a certain age who has reached a certain station in life as it were, someone with purchasing power. And the people with the purchasing power are likely to be people who identify with senior golf and senior golfers.

'I think it's great that the game has become as popular as it has, that we're building golf courses all over the world, doing all these wonderful things. And some of the technical aspects of the game are great, but we have to be very, very careful. I think we have to be careful that we educate the golfer, the new golfer as to the traditions and etiquette of the game of golf, or it will lose one of its most valuable aspects which is that it is a traditional game, a game for all people to enjoy. We should provide facilities and academies for the beginner golfer so that he understands the tradition and etiquette. Whether he is from St Andrews, or New York City, or Tokyo, these are the resonsibilities of every golfer to keep the game as we have known it.'

The Other Side of the Coin

If the tournament life meant the good life for Jacklin, it has meant a life of luxury for his successors at the top of the game. Ian Woosnam has a private aeroplane. Greg Norman has a stable of performance cars and when he wants to get away from it all . . .

'It's easy – I have a beautiful sports fishing boat filled with sports fishing gear. I have a wonderful captain and a first mate who loves to dive, and I just disappear, to Mexico or the Virgin Islands in the Caribbean, or to the Bahamas, and scuba dive. That is my relaxation. I forget everything when I dive to 130 feet. It's my freedom. No one can bother you there. I love it with a passion just as much as playing golf.'

Arnold Palmer, in his sixties, finds his annual net worth appreciating by several million dollars, thanks to the contracts and investments he has made, and to the sponsorships and agencies which he still has. Jack Nicklaus turns over, at least, several million dollars each year in the golf course design business. The world of Ballesteros and Faldo and Lyle and Woosnam and Olazabal is the tip of the iceberg –

out in the sun. The vast bulk of the tournament world is still beneath the waves – very much in the shadow of the great stars. That's where the Tony Charnleys of the golfing world live.

Tony Charnley was born on Christmas Day, 1954, in Derbyshire. By the time he was 20, he knew he wanted to be a professional golfer. So he became one. In his first full year in competition, his official prize money was £39. After 16 years on the tournament circuit, Tony had not won a single tournament. In 1991, Rodger Davis of Australia, who finished ninth in the Order of Merit that season, won more prize money than Tony, who finished ninety-fifth, had won in his entire career. The figures were £350 312 to £345 798. Tony Charnley lives in the real world, light years distant from that of Woosnam and Faldo and Ballesteros and Norman.

A few seasons into his career, Tony met Lucienne, a Dutch girl whom he married in 1981. When they started, as Tony explained,

'We didn't have enough money for the two of us to travel on tour, flying everywhere, so we bought a camper vehicle. We were not sure about it, but we used it for two years, went to every tournament in it for two years. One or two players had caravans, but most of them flew from one venue to the next. There was a travel agency arranging things for pros then, but we couldn't afford it.

'The money has changed dramatically. In 1980, I finished in the top ten for the first time and won £750 in the Dutch Open. A month later, I finished second in Germany, and won £3700. If I did the same today, I would win £65 000.

'I never really made a living, it was like I was just keeping going. But the tour gets to be part of your life. I like it … I wouldn't be doing it 12 years later if I didn't, so I guess it's part of me now, till what age I don't know.'

Tony Charnley is a vintage optimist. Perhaps he has to be.

'I actually feel my game is getting better. For a long time I played not really knowing much about the golf swing. I just played off feelings, where now I have learned over the last five years a lot about my own swing. I like the challenge of golf – that one day you decide you have mastered the game, and the next day you can go out and find yourself saying, "Why did I ever think I had mastered this game?" The game has got its own back on you again. The game changes from day to day. There is something about this golf, it just gets a hold of you.'

CHAPTER THREE

PLAYGROUND MANAGEMENT

.

The Royal and Ancient Golf Club of St Andrews and the United States Golf Association govern the game of golf throughout the world. Their concerns are for the millions of amateur golfers and their wellbeing in terms of how the Rules of Golf will affect them, of defining clearly 'amateur status'. These are their main concerns, but the march of time has brought other responsibilities: promoting championships, making grants to federations, associations, clubs, educational institutes, the only proviso being the advancement of the game, and the maintenance of its health and vigour. Then there are the professional golfers' associations, which are trade associations concerned with the working conditions and circumstances of golf professionals retained by clubs. As the objectives and profile of the club professional and the tournament player became more diverse it became clear that they could no longer exist under one roof. Thus were two of the most remarkable organizations in the history of the sport born: the US PGA Tour and the European PGA Tour.

John Jacobs was born in Lindrick, Yorkshire in 1925. He was born to golf. His father had been a club professional, his mother a club stewardess. In time, he became professional at the Sandy Lodge Club, near London, and in the nineteen fifties, played in such tournaments as existed, a dozen or so each year. He made the Ryder Cup team at Palm Springs in 1955 and achieved some notoriety as the only British player in the history of the event with a 100 per cent record. At that time, all the professional events in the British Isles, save for the Open Championship were controlled by the PGA, which had an executive committee of 28 made up of senior and respected club professionals. In addition, as part of the existing schedule, there were one or two open championships on the Continent, each controlled by their national federations. Jacobs, with a few other players, prominent among them Peter Alliss, Bernard Hunt and David Thomas, who were the first of the British 'tournament' players as such, felt that they should have a positive voice in the running of these events, and sought representation on the committee, with a view to setting up a separate tournament organization. After much agitation, they were conceded four places to represent the tournament players! In that regard, Jacobs' day was to come.

He drifted out of tournament play, becoming increasingly interested in, and successful at, teaching, and was soon spending much of his time in Europe, retained by the various national associations to show their professionals how to teach. Subsequently, he became managing director of a company which built and operated driving ranges and par three courses, and was active in television commentary. By 1963, Jacobs had susbtantially finished with competitive golf and was concentrating on teaching and business.

In 1972, John Bywaters, secretary of the PGA approached him and asked if he would like to try to expand the British tour. Recalling his past experience with the executive committee, his first instinct was to say, 'No thank you very much.' He was very busy with other things. But the more he thought about it, the more he thought, 'Well, I can do this. Perhaps I owe it to the game.' When Bywaters came back to him, he said: 'If you can get me a contract which gives me an absolutely free hand, I'll do it. But I can only do it for 50 per cent of my time because I've got to run these golf centres, and I am teaching all the European amateur teams.' John persuaded the powers that be to allow Jacobs to do it, and gave him a contract that gave him a free hand.

'I was appointed in September 1971. By Christmas it was obvious to me that there was no way I could expand the British tour because Great Britain is such a small country. You couldn't have the best players playing only one hundred miles from where they had been the week before. And since I knew all the people in golf in Europe – people who were running the French Open, the Spanish Open and so on – I very quickly saw that it was time to broaden the market. At that time only the very wealthy played in most of these countries, so that it was the start of a fairly long process. But an awful lot has happened in the past twenty years. Sevvy Ballesteros has appeared, which means the game has taken off and spanned out on the Continent. Bernhard Langer has appeared in Germany, Swedish players are coming out, and a lot of good players have come through so that the game is percolating downwards to the masses as it did here and in the States.

'Without really planning it, we have followed pretty closely what was happening in the States. The tournament players have taken over the tournament game, putting their own administrative structures on it, and so on. I played on the American Tour as it was in 1955–56, really to have a break from standing teaching all winter in our wretched weather, and I'm sure what I saw affected my thinking. When I took on the tournaments, they were sponsored by companies in the golf trade, ball manufacturers like Penfold, people like Swallow rainwear, Dunlop and so on. But the prize money was abysmal.

'I wrote to all these existing sponsors and said that in the future there would have to be a minimum prize fund for a tournament. No such thing existed. If a week was empty, someone just put up a few hundred pounds and they would play for that. The minimum would be £8000, and £15 000 for certain periods of the year. That would mean that ten or twelve of the players would make some money, some would break even, and all the rest would lose money, as opposed to the existing system in which everybody except the first four or five lost money! The result of that was that I very smartly lost two sponsors the first month I was in business expanding the British tour! But those first few months, from September to Christmas, were unbelievably successful. And I think merely the creation of the post, of telling the world that Jacobs was there to try to develop the thing meant that people came to me. I didn't realize at the time, but looking back, knowing all these people on the Continent was the key.

'One other critical factor was Tony Jacklin, who had won the Open Championship in 1969 and the US Open in 1970; these two major championships in a spell of eleven months. Jacklin was the best player in the world at the time. The existing prize money was not good enough to keep him playing in Europe. So without any compunction I made two rules: one was that anyone who had won a major championship could negotiate appearance money with tournament sponsors. This Jacklin was able to do with Mark McCormack and his management team. The other rule was that during certain weeks in the year, none of our players could play elsewhere in the world, without my permission. These were the four or five weeks around the Open Championship, then in the autumn – September time.'

The 'Jacklin Rule' about appearance money became a rod for the infant tour's back and, twenty years on, it lingers in a rather shadowy fashion. In the late seventies, the European Tour brought in a rule putting an end to appearance money. Severiano Ballesteros won the Open Championship in 1979 and the US Masters in 1980, and he wanted appearance money. He was, it might be said, out of favour with the Tour people, but he argued not without reason that Americans such as Lee Trevino, Tom Weiskopf and others were coming in and being paid appearance money. Jacobs asked to speak to the Tour committee and said that he agreed to putting an end to appearance money, but that realistically having done it for Jacklin and considering why it had been done for him, they could scarcely stop Ballesteros from having appearance money. The committee turned him down, and Ballesteros did not play in the 1981 Ryder Cup team, a source of great irritation to Jacobs, who captained the teams of 1979 and 1981. Severiano Ballesteros was the best player in the world at the time and Jacobs fought to have him selected. Ballesteros probably still thinks that it was John Jacobs, the team captain, who kept him out.

Severiano Ballesteros winning the first of his five major championships, the 1979 Open at Royal Lytham & St Annes.

Jacobs left the European Tournament Players' Division, as it was then known in 1975. He went off to develop the John Jacobs Golf Academy concept, very successfully, in the United States. Ken Schofield, one of the staff, was appointed executive director in the same year, of what eventually became the PGA European Tour. Under his direction, the European Tour has divorced itself completely from the PGA, and has extended the boundaries of its tournaments beyond Europe into North Africa and the Middle East and even to Thailand. The political and economic consolidation of the European Community throughout the seventies and the boom decade of the eighties made it a success story. Total prize money exceeded £1 million in 1977, £2 million in 1982, and by 1992 was touching £20 million. Some 24 nations are represented by the players each year, with some 500 young men trying to qualify for a place on the Tour each year.

Schofield, takes a good deal of pleasure from the fact that his American counterpart is almost an exact contemporary in terms of years on the job, and has had many of the same experiences.

The US PGA Tour

Deane Beman, Commissioner of the US PGA Tour.

Deane R. Beman, who was born in Washington DC in 1938, brings a high class pedigree to the office of chief executive, or Commissioner as the position is called, of the PGA Tour, as the Americans have it. As a player, he won the British Amateur Championship in 1959, the US Amateur in 1960 and 1963, played on four Walker Cup teams, four World Amateur Championship teams and three Americas Cup teams. In 1967, aged 29, he left an insurance brokerage firm in Bethesda, Washington, to become a tour professional. In six years on the tour, he won four events before becoming Commissioner in 1974. Beman has been a controversial figure. But then incumbents of all such posts are apt to be. But his achievement for the PGA Tour is staggering. When Beman joined the organization, its assets were $730 000. By 1992, they were in the region of a breathtaking $175 million.

The US Tour had its origins, romantically, in the 'Grapefruit Circuit'. When winter came to the northern states and snow was thick on the ground, clubs would close and golf professionals would head south. A few tournaments sprang up, at Florida resorts mainly, and although there was not a great deal of money involved, competition was keen as the professionals kept their games in shape, their feet dry and warm, and the resorts got some publicity. Often the wives would organize the events. Of course in those early days they were all club professionals, not tournament pros. There were summer tournaments, of course, such as the Western Open in the Chicago area and the Metropolitan Open in New York. As well as the US Open and from 1916 the US PGA.

April 1 would be a seasonal turning point, when most of the northern clubs would re-open. On the way north, there might be an event or two in the mid-Atlantic states, such as the North and South at Pinehurst. By the thirties, the PGA of America was becoming involved in a rather arm's length way, but these were the beginnings of a more regular tour. Walter Hagen had shown the way to other players by becoming probably the first professional who could make a living purely out of tournaments and the accompanying exhibition matches. The PGA didn't actually conduct the events themselves.

They might send an official to officiate and give rules decisions and the like, but the tournaments were invariably run by local organizations.

Bob Harlow, manager in his day of Walter Hagen, was the first PGA tournament director, with a brief to bring some order into the schedule, and when he left to found *Golf World*, the weekly golf magazine, he was succeeded by Fred Corcoran, from Cambridge, Massachusetts, where his father had been a groundsman at Harvard University. As glib and lively as any of the Boston Irish, Corcoran hustled, moving ahead of the tour speaking to community groups and extolling the benefits that a PGA tournament could bring to the town, and above all making friends with the press. In these pre-television days, the golf writers and radio men were kings. Before he left, Corcoran raised the prize money to close on $1 million and laid the foundations of a burgeoning organization.

The Junior Chamber of Commerce structure is one of the great fund-raising organizations in America, and they were and are very much involved in sponsoring golf tournaments for charity. The Los Angeles Open, which dates from the very early twenties is run by the Jaycees, as the Chambers of Commerce are known, as were Greensboro, Hartford and others. The Western Golf Association, with its Western Open, has raised huge sums for the Evans Scholarship Foundation, created by Chic Evans to put caddies through school. There are 800 students in schools through Evans Scholarships. This charitable element exists largely because in the United States this is the most tax efficient method of sponsoring golf tournaments, but it is also one of which Deane Beman is rightly proud.

'We have almost all of our tournaments run for charity, 100 per cent of the net proceeds of the events go to charity. We have tax exempt foundations, local organizations putting together the volunteers, providing the sponsorship, going out and getting commercial sponsorship and contracting with the PGA Tour to run these events. In the last few years we have been raising somewhere in the neighbourhood of $20-$25 million a year for the local charities that are represented by the volunteers in these local civic organizations. That is really the backbone of how this tour works and why professional tournament golf works.

'In earlier years, up to perhaps the mid-seventies, the local organizations were responsible for the administration of the event, raising the money, selling the tickets, all that. We would simply send in our officials to officiate at the competition on competition days only. Now things are quite different. All the functions that were done locally are still done locally, but the PGA Tour now gets more involved. For instance our agronomy staff does a great deal of advance work with the golf course superintendent to prepare the ground for the competition.

'The PGA Tour is now deeply involved in actually assisting directly the tournament organization which is raising the local money for the event. Helping them to finance the dollars necessary for a major event today. A budget for a tournament today, with a $1 million purse, is somewhere between $2.5 million and $4 million to put on the event. And that may be beyond the ability of the local organization to raise the money locally. So we've brought in the concept of title sponsorship on the back of television contracts which we negotiate nationally and which generate somewhere between 35 and 40 per cent of all prize money that is won in tournaments today. This is passed on to the local people to help the event succeed. In addition we have marketing arrangements with companies like Coca-Cola and IBM and Delta Airlines, National Car Rental and major licensing contracts that provide additional funding, not only to local sponsors, but for our player health insurance and our player pension plan. So the whole thing is a much more complicated and comprehensive business than it was in the early days.

'There is great interest in our Tour. The United States is so much larger in area, and we have those big population centres. So the Tour goes to more diverse cities. In Japan for instance, I guess that half of the tournaments are played between Osaka and Tokyo. In the States, we go to the northeast in the summertime, to the mid-west in the summer and in the fall we start moving south. In winter we go out west and southwest, then back to Florida. So we're covering many, many more cities, reaching more people. Actually the galleries we get – the people who are out there and can touch the players – are far more than the other tours. The size of our operation is surprising.

'Of course, we are now operating three tours. The traditional Tour as we have all known it for 50 years is now matched by the Senior Tour, which is now as large as the traditional Tour was when I came here. It has a full schedule of over 40 events, requiring its own staff, and there is now the Ben Hogan Tour, for younger players, with 30 events. So we have three separate staffs;

three separate tours with approximately 120 events in something like 110 or 115 cities.

'The Tour is much bigger than the money. Most of the activities we are engaged in, we'd still do, even if they didn't generate any income. For example we have PGA Tour Productions, which is our television arm, and which brings to the world more information about golf and our players. It also assists us in promoting the game of golf itself. Then there is PGA Tour Investments Inc. which handles our golf course programme. We have now 17 golf clubs that we own and operate. The first one being the Tournament Players' Club at Sawgrass, our headquarters. The courses are built for the specific purpose of conducting a golf tournament, with built-in spectator areas. These courses are of major assistance to sponsors in conducting a more successful event.'

Deane Beman has been severely criticized for being too parochial in the sense that he shows no concern for the other world tours, and has been obstructive and some might consider antagonistic on the subject of American players playing in Europe and elsewhere outside the United States when American tournaments are being played. He has a forceful response to such charges:

'It is a very complicated question. I believe there is always the recognition that if players are able to move around and compete worldwide, that is in the interest of players, in the interest of golf worldwide. So we take that as a premise and I don't believe that any of the associations at any time have ever said our players can't go anywhere and play. Then you get down to the judgement of how much flexibility can we provide for the players in our association and still fulfil our obligations to the sponsors that we contract with to make our livelihood on a week to week basis. And there is the rub ... the judgement we have here, and I've been in this position for 19 years, is that well up to 96, 97, 98 per cent of the time, anytime a US player wants to go anywhere in the world to play, we have approved. There are very few instances when we have not been able to provide that flexibility.

'The same attitude exists with players coming here to play. Now you have to have rules or you don't have a game, you have to have rules for players coming in to compete, being able to compete, being able to leave competing, or you don't have a tour. You can't make a contract with television or tournament sponsors – we do have very flexible rules, I think. Some individuals would like more flexibility, no question about that. But I think that the rules are flexible and reasonable and any player who wishes to play internationally today, can. But where their home tour is involved, they have to have a certain obligation to support those events or the events wouldn't be there. They wouldn't be there for the opportunity for someone else to come in and play there. I think we are fairly close to a system that is in balance.'

The European PGA Tour

The European Tour takes a more liberal, more discursive view of exchanges, under the guidance of Ken Schofield. In many ways, his organization has followed the Beman example and achievement, which has been possible in an economy, that through the eighties at least, saw sponsors galore anxious to capitalize on golf's power as a marketing tool. The Europeans too have entered the field of direct television negotiations with the broadcasters on a tourwide basis, and are active in developing a golf course property division. Schofield sees his executive mandate clearly. It is to:

Ken Schofield, Executive Director of the Eurpean PGA Tour.

'obtain tournaments for our members to play in with prize money incentives which make them worthwhile. We encourage the best of the rest of the nations to join us and regularly we have players from 24 nations competing on our tour. We go back to the days when players like Norman von Nida, Peter Thomson, Kel Nagle, Bobby Locke, Gary Player and all the Commonwealth golfers played here. Greg Norman for example will tell you that he cut his teeth in Britain and in the Continental Opens. Our policy then, back in the fifties and sixties, was to welcome the best players and that tradition continues.

'Now we have Rodger Davis from Australia, Mark McNulty from Zimbabwe, Eduardo Romero from Argentina and many others. We welcome this. We want our players to support the European tour. It is their tour after all, for all of them, not just a few superstars. But at the same time, players who want to play internationally, to be competitive at the very top of the game – Faldo, Lyle, Woosnam, Ballesteros, Langer, Olazabal and a few others – must have an opportunity to play in the States. That's right and proper. And we can accommodate American players who want to join us. Payne Stewart, for example, spent quite a few weeks playing in European events in 1991. The US Tour system I believe requires their players to commit to 15 events on their circuit. This gives them releases to play events outside the US Tour. If they play five more US events, they have additional releases. So I imagine we should see more and more US players playing in certain European events.'

The return of South Africa to full participation in international sport may have a very positive effect on world golf. Such countries as Sweden, Holland, Spain, Canada and of course all the African countries, had outlawed South African golfers. Now they will be free to play anywhere. With a programme of events which runs from January to March, it might fit very well with the European schedule, which really starts in earnest from 1 March, in Spain. The result of all this action could well see the European Tour enlarged.

This expansion would suggest that the concept of a 'world tour', which many of the game's personalities have discussed albeit infor-

Jose Maria Olazabal, one of the stars who enabled the European PGA Tour to grow in stature during the 1980s, at play in the Volvo PGA Championship at Wentworth.

mally, is at the very least a possibility. There are intriguing arguments for it, principally that only during perhaps four weeks each year, the weeks of the majors, do all the best players in the world have a chance to play against each other. Even that is modified by qualification systems. And in the case of the Masters, a smaller field than the others is entirely at the mercy of invitations from a private club. Each of the other majors has its own governing body none of which incidentally are under the auspices of any of the PGA Tours. What would be required would be some kind of overall world administrative body, but where that is to come from is the rub. Each of the world's major tours, the US, Europe, Japan and to a lesser extent Australia, is essentially provincial; a trade association concerned inevitably with protecting the interests of its members.

Deane Beman's PGA Tour for instance has 250 card-carrying members each with the same vote, all of whom Beman must satisfy, so that the 'Mediocre Majority' as the US writers called them, have more control over policy than the stars which the galleries pay to watch. But the US Federal Trades Commission is investigating the PGA Tour policy of requiring a player to have an official release from Beman if he wants to play in a tournament anywhere else in the world the same week as a PGA Tour event. This protectionism may be found illegal in terms of 'restraint of trade'. Matters could also be complicated further by the American 1RS changing the tax laws allowing sponsorship money to be taken before tax, if charitable donations are part of the package. All in all the 1990s could see a number of changes in the accountable structure of world professional golf.

The Seniors Tours

The Senior PGA Tour, considered by many to be the single most successful sports development of the eighties and by any standard a complete phenomenon, was the outcome of an informal meeting in 1979, when a few of the older tournament players met to discuss the possibilities. Attending the meeting were Sam Snead, Julius Boros, Gardner Dickinson, Bob Goalby, Don January and the late Dan Sikes, all of them experienced tournament players and winners, with significant reputations in the game. Snead was named honorary chairman, and Sikes was appointed chairman of what became known as the Senior Advisory Council. Sponsors were found and the US PGA Tour agreed to administer the new schedule. Two tournaments were held in 1980: one in Atlantic City, one in Florida. There were five events in 1981, 11 in 1982, and 18 in 1983, when total prize money was more than $3 million. In the early years, one Arnold Palmer arrived on the senior scene, and promptly won five tournaments.

By 1985, the new tour was large enough, with 27 events worth over $6 million, to require a separate division inside the PGA Tour attending to its own operations and financing, with an extended board of directors. In 1985, Peter Thomson of Australia won no fewer than nine tournaments and ten events in a 12-month stretch. A new senior entry was Gary Player. The pro-am element of these senior events was strongly emphasized and was a critical selling point to sponsors. The attraction to business was that here was the opportunity for corporate decisionmakers to play with their boyhood heroes. Such has been the growth of the Seniors that in 1990 Lee Trevino became the leading money winner with a total of $1 190 518, greater than any other golfer on any other tour in the entire world.

Bottom left:
Don January and his wife with the US Seniors PGA Cup in 1982.

Below:
For the professional life now begins at 50. **Gary Player** and **Arnold Palmer** chatting during a Seniors tournament at Turnberry in 1990.

Japan

While all this was going on in the west, things were stirring in the inscrutable east. The first golf course in Japan, the Kobe Golf Club, dates from 1903, and was started by English tea merchant, Arthur Groom, and friends. Almost all the early clubs were patronized by foreigners. The Tokyo Golf Club, at Komazawa, was the first club formed by the Japanese for the Japanese, in 1914.

The game prospered through the twenties and thirties, when top American professionals such as Walter Hagen, Bill Melhorn and Bobby Cruickshank visited, as did the British golf architect Charles Alison. Golf was very much a game for the élite, virtually unknown to the mass of the population, but the Japanese Golf Association was formed in 1924 (by five Japanese, six foreigners and with a constitution written in English!). The Japanese PGA was set up in 1926 and that same year, the first professional tournament, the Kansai Open, was played. The next year, the first Open Championship of Japan was played at Hodogaya Country Club near Yokohama, and was won by an amateur Rukoro Asaboshi, with 309. By 1933, Tomekichi Miya-moto felt ready to tackle the Open Championship at St Andrews, the first Japanese professional so to do.

Japan's first major golf boom followed the victory of Torakichi Nakamura and Koichi Ono for Japan in the 1957 Canada (now World) Cup. It has persisted ever since, marching in step with the extraordinary Japanese economy itself. Now the unique structure of the game there supports a staggering professional tour approaching $27 million in prize money and 83 tournaments; a startling illustration of the economic power of this nation of more than 100 million people crammed into islands not much larger than the British Isles of which four-fifths is mountainous and uninhabitable. The Japanese Tour is sustained by massive media coverage by television, radio and the written word, and by the sponsorship of some of the most impressive corporations in the world. Visits in the sixties by the big three of Arnold Palmer, Gary Player and Jack Nicklaus, and since then players like Tom Watson and Severiano Ballesteros, have maintained the growth of the game in Japan.

With that kind of schedule and money available, there is simply little incentive for Japanese professionals to travel abroad to earn a crust. Jumbo Ozaki, Japan's number one, earned more than 100 million yen or $780 000 in each year of 1988, 1989, 1990. The most famous Japanese golfer internationally, Isao Aoki, won the Suntory World Match Play in 1978, the Hawaiian Open and the European Open in 1983 and the Coca-Cola Classic in 1989, confirming him as a world figure and the only Japanese golfer to win in the west. Surprisingly, Japanese women pros have been more successful overseas. Chako Higuchi won the Australian Women's Open in 1974, the Colgate European Open in 1976 and the US LPGA Championship in 1977. Ayako Okamoto has topped the US LPGA Money List and won 16 tournaments in the USA.

The number of golfers in Japan is loosely talked of as being 15 million or 20 million – it depends what you mean by 'golfer'. The number of golfers using golf courses per annum is put at 11.3 million; the number using driving ranges, of which there are 4970 registered in Japan, is put at 13.6 million. Golfers at golf courses spend an average of $103 per visit, those at driving ranges $14. One of the most coveted possessions for the Japanese golfer is membership of a club, although this is made purely as a financial investment. Except for a very few British-type clubs, which can be joined only through special introductions, if at all, membership of a Japanese golf club depends solely on wealth.

One of the most successful Japanese women golfers worldwide, **Ayoko Okamoto** during the World Championship of Women's Golf in 1990.

Left: Pressure on space restricts many Japanese to driving ranges.

The Japanese golf club membership market reached an unrealistic high in 1987, came down some months later, and steadied. The most expensive club continues to be Tokyo's Koganei, designed by Walter Hagen, dating from 1932 and costing $2.48 million! It is a system that encourages abuse. Recently there was an advertisement in a newspaper offering membership in a new golf club for 2 500 000 yen, about £10 000. In Japan there are very many people who can afford that kind of money for a golf membership. But the advertiser had not specified the number of memberships available – he accepted 55 000! He was about to make a vast amount of money, but was unmasked, and very smartly arrested.

Nowadays, golf in Japan is high fashion. It has taken the place of tennis as the most trendy sport for teenagers and young women. Going to a driving range with your date in an expensive car, then having a few drinks at a favourite pub with golf clubs in hand (status symbol!) is now a favoured way to spend an evening. And for Japan's busy 'sararimen' (salaried workers), golf has an entirely different meaning. Being a better-than-average golfer may not only speed promotion, but it is a useful asset in conducting negotiations and advancing one's business and social status and connections. It is normal for a new male employee to buy a set of golf clubs with his first bonus. For the Japanese, golf represents an escape from the pressures of daily life and the chance to enjoy nature in what is a heavily urbanized society. And for the golf professional and professional golfer alike, Japan is by way of being a Shangri-la.

Japan is the only major golfing nation where the tournament players and club professionals live contentedly under one administrative roof. Elsewhere, as we have seen, the Tours have spun themselves off from the older club pros' bodies and achieved a high profile, multi-million dollar status, far more glamorous in many ways than the organizations of their origins.

But, the old PGAs of Britain and America live on in their shadow, performing very much the function they were originally set up to do. First and foremost, they are trade associations, bodies to serve the interests of their members, the club pros. They run competitions for these lesser golfing lights and provide training in all those areas of business essential to the successful running of a pro's shop.

Peter Alliss was of course one of Britain's premier tournament players prior to his even more high profile existence in television, but with his father a professional before him, he grew up in that world:

'I still fervently believe in them, and I still believe there are far worse ways of making a living. To go to a nice place is a tremendous bonus instead of a horrid factory. Even the most modest of clubs is usually in the best part of town. Usually you're meeting people who are receptive to having their leisure time, so they're not antagonistic. You, on the other hand, must never have a headache, never have any family problems. You never had Aunt Nellie die and she promised you she'd leave you something in the will, and the dog's been run over. You're rather like a publican, or a restaurateur or a maître d'. You smile and hope people give you money. You are in the "love me" business, and the "love me" business can be quite tedious.'

So what of the ladies in all this? For all the same reasons that kept women from being accepted in the work place, the arrival of professional women golfers came long after the men. As was the case with the men, acceptance and emancipation came first in America. Babe Zaharias, after her Olympic gold medal winning career, turned to golf after the war and professional golf at that. There was very little for her to play in and she tried to break down further barriers when she came to Britain in the 1940s. Bobby Burnet recalls her visit.

'In 1947, Babe Zaharias came over and won our Ladies Open Championship at Gullane that year. She was a fantastic player and she wanted to enter our Open Championship and her entry was turned down. Well, I suppose it would have established a precedent if they had allowed her in, but that was a pity because her favourite pastime was outdriving American Walker Cup players. She would go out on the course and hit it 50 yards past them, which didn't please them very much. At one hole at Gullane, a par five of 540 yards, she reached the green with a drive and a 5 iron.'

Professional ladies' golf really got going in the States after the war. By 1980, prize money on their circuit had risen to $5 million and has risen steadily ever since, peaking in 1992 at over $21 million. In terms of profile, the middle 1980s was their best time, when Nancy Lopez and Pat Bradley were so successful, that they were only second and third respectively to Curtis Strange in the 1985 world money earnings.

More recently, they have struggled for television exposure as the men's Senior Tour has become such a glamorous entity with Nicklaus and Trevino now playing alongside the likes of Palmer, Player and Rodriguez.

Today, the women's professional game is not that much different to where the men were 30 years ago. There are women's tours in other parts of the world, most notably Europe and Japan, but to gain world recognition and truly substantial rewards, it is necessary to camp on the American circuit. The first contest between Europe and America in the Solheim Cup, also resembled the pattern of so many Ryder Cups down the years – somewhat onesided in favour of America.

Babe Zaharias, the Olympic gold medal winner, and to many the originator of women's professional golf.

Nancy Lopez and Pat Bradley, two of the most successful women golfers of all time.

CHAPTER FOUR

In Pursuit
Of Perfection

.

The Coaches

Bobby Jones had Stewart Maiden. Jack Niclaus had Jack Grout.
Arnold Palmer never had one. Ben Hogan, Byron Nelson and Sam
Snead never had one. The idea that any of these champions needed
'spiritual teaching', or guidance in 'matters of fundamental intellectual
concern' might have had them reaching for a niblick. But then the
word 'guru' as it relates to golf teachers is simply media licence, descri-
bing golf instructors who have worked at tuning the swings of highly
talented tournament players, and champions.

The cynics would say that any successful 'guru' is one who has
hitched his wagon to a star, latched on to a golfer who would in any
case be a winner, and that a measure of the guru's success relates to
the titles and prize-money won by his 'pupil'. And certainly, life being
as it is, when Nick Faldo in 1990 won both the Masters and the Open
Championship, and became the best player in the world however
briefly, David Leadbetter, his mentor, was hailed as a kind of messiah.

Leadbetter will teach anyone, from beginners upwards, although
for a duffer, his one-hour lesson might well be as much as $300. But
in the case of Faldo, he was not teaching the man how to play golf, he
was helping him re-cast his swing. After all, the man had been the
leading money winner in Europe in 1983, with a dozen tournament
wins behind him, Ryder Cup appearances and top ten finishes in the
Open Championship. No, Nick Faldo simply wanted to win the Open,
and be the best, as Leadbetter explained:

'We sought to put a little more body action into his swing. To start
with, Nick has very long legs. He was very much, I'd say, an arms
and legs player and, as a result, was fairly "handsy" through the
ball. He tended to have a rather upright swing, used to slide his
legs a lot and then simply time his hand release through the ball.
What we have really done is simplify his swing. He doesn't have

Team Faldo!

nearly as steep a plane as he had, he's certainly flattened it, and timed the release with his body, so that his body is now really controlling how his hands come in.

'Nick Faldo's swing relied so much on rhythm. More than anything else, his angle of attack as we call it, the angle at which the club came down on the ball, would be fairly steep. As a result, he would apply a fairly lofted trajectory to his shots. Now if he was playing in the wind, downwind was not so much a problem, but into wind, he had very little piercing flight on his shots. His main goal at the time was to win the Open and he needed to flight the ball. If you are talking links golf, you are talking wind. If you want to play well in the wind, you have to flight the ball. Nick was very inconsistent into the wind and in controlling the distance he hit with each iron. That was the thinking behind it all.

'I suppose understanding the golf swing is probably 25 per cent of a teacher's duty. The other 75 per cent is communication, explaining to people how they should feel about their action. I try to impart drills and exercises so that the students are able to feel what goes on in the swing. Those little drills and exercises that Nick's always doing enable him to have that feel, especially when he is on the course. Everybody has a certain feel when one gets on the tee – that this feels good, that the swing is going to be good that day. And these drills help Nick to feel that way.

'Things have evolved a lot over the years really. With the advent of video, people can see what happens in their golf swing and teachers are able to analyse what goes on. With the change of equipment and of golf courses all the time, we are coming to two types of instruction: one for the better player, another for the average club golfer. There is no question these days that the tournament players are really athletes, stronger and generally younger than they were. So it's a case of being able to adapt to teaching a style which allows them to play day in and day out, injury free, but also to their full potential.

'When we worked with Seve, we were really fine tuning little things and trying to give him a different sensation. He is such a natural player that what with his elasticity or flexibility or what-ever you want to term it, I felt that he had allowed a little too much hip turn to creep into his swing, and was losing what I call the "taut" in his swing. The comparison is stretching a rubber band then letting it go, and I felt that he was tending to swing back and swing through without really very much "taut". Part of that may have had to do with his back problems.

'What we did was to restrict his hip turn. I used to get behind him and almost try to pull his left hip towards me as he started back, so it gives him a much tighter feeling of what he needs. The other thing was that because of this excessive hip turn, I felt he was getting very narrow coming to the ball. We've all seen how his head goes backward around impact, and sometimes he will block the shot or hook the ball. I wanted him to feel that he was getting "wider" as he came down to the ball, so I would stand behind him and as he started down push his hands in towards his body. He would resist, try to push me the opposite way, and widen his swing. Once in Japan we did this a few times and almost immediately he started to hit the ball with much more solidity. It gave him a lot of confidence.

'He has a couple of things to ponder over. We just keep check-ing. It's not a case of making major changes with Seve. . . . I love his golf. He's got fantastic rhythm. He sets up to the ball beautifully. Everybody is always learning little things about their game, as they get older. Seve is probably not as strong as he was ten, or twelve years ago and he might have to change his swing accordingly. I've always felt the older you get the better your swing techniques should be, because you're not relying on pure physical strength and ability to get by.'

'You could say that Jack Nicklaus had the first really modern swing. He developed a technique that used the big muscles to a great extent – a wide one-piece takeaway, a tremendous pivot in which he'd wind his shoulders round 100 degrees, coil up like a spring, then use his lower body to impart amazing speed to the ball. It was amazing how far he hit the ball. Very much like Norman in this day and age. A little bit like Ian Woosnam as well. Greg Norman has a power swing, which is maybe not totally suited to an iron type of swing. If Greg has any shortcomings whatsoever, I would say they were in his iron play.

'Jack Nicklaus set the trend for teaching in the sixties, as Hogan had done in the fifties, and the Nicklaus-Norman type swing seems to have come round a bit in the last few years. Ben Hogan was a law unto himself. His flexibility was unbelievable, the things he could do. You have to remember that he was not a particularly tall man, and he would stand fairly erect to the ball. Now I think we have sort of hit on a happy medium in which we are trying to put people on a swing plane that really suits them. The end result, the bottom line as the Americans say, is that we are trying to create a repeating golf swing. And I believe the way that we can do that for the better players is to keep the hand action to a minimum.

'In teaching, the big thing is that you are looking at a player's ability. If people see me teaching a particular player, they may say, "Well, David Leadbetter teaches this." But what I do is to try to maintain some kind of versatility whereby my teaching can suit all levels of players. You may grip the club and set up to the ball like a Nick Faldo, and be the same size as Nick. But if your life is such that you play only once every two weeks, and don't have time to practise, you might not be in the best physical shape to try a golf swing which is based on the use of big muscles. If we really got you to wind up and tore a back muscle, you would not be too happy. So we would try to create a swing for you with a little bit more of a hands-and-arms motion through the ball. Some players are just not strong enough to do what Faldo does.'

From time to time, David Leadbetter has worked with Scott Simpson, Larry Mize, Wayne Grady, Nick Price, David Frost and Mark McNulty as well as Faldo and, briefly, Ballesteros – an impressive array of clients. The whole business of the 'guru' probably started 20 years ago with Bob Toski, a successful tour player who turned to teaching. A Toski associate in the past is Peter Kostis, who is credited with bringing a sports psychologist, Dr Bob Rotella, into the ring. Now Rotella works with several of the American tour players, as Alan Fine does in the UK. Kostis has a very precise view of his teaching philosophy:

'You talk about the evolution of the golf swing vis-á-vis equipment and the golf course, but there has been an extraordinary change in the evolution of the teaching of the golf swing. My method, if I have one, is that I am dealing strictly and solely with the individual that I am looking at, at that particular time. I just don't believe that there is one swing for everybody, but I believe that everybody needs one swing. Therefore when I work with a Mark Calcavecchia, say, I need to know Mark. I need to know him inside out. I need to know his psychological makeup, his personality. I need to know his physical limitations, his strengths and weaknesses, so that we can construct for him a golf swing that he can really rely on under all kinds of pressure. That's the basis on which I work with everyone. In terms of Mark, he is what we can call a right brain player.

'You can divide golfers into right brain, left brain. Right brainers are a little more creative, artistic. So long as they are playing well, they feel the swing is OK. The left brainers are the analytical ones, the drivers, the mechanics. They must have swing confidence in order to play with confidence. And I would deal with a Mark Calcavecchia entirely differently to a Bernhard Langer. So Mark and I play a lot of golf. We do spend time working on his fundamentals because they are important. We will hit balls on the range, and I try to give him drills and exercises that are fun, because to a right brainer it is absolutely the most painful thing in the world to stand there and hit a series of poorly-struck golf shots. They are so shot-orientated that I have to put him in an environment where he can disregard the flight of the ball. So we put it all in the form of a drill, or a game.

'When it comes to a major championship or a Ryder Cup, there is not a whole lot you can do once the players are at the venue. It's fine tuning then, confirmation that what is being done is fine, so get on with it. The player may have a couple of lingering questions that need to be answered, but there is no major work that can be done. If anyone goes into a Ryder Cup competition with concern about his golf swing, then you can chalk that point up to the opposition. You'd better have your swing in order before you get there.

'Just as Calcavecchia is a right brain person, Nick Faldo for example is a left brain person. He needs swing confidence in order to have play confidence. Tom Kite is like that, Bernhard Langer is like that. So at that final moment, when they go into the tournament or on to the tee, they are looking for a little swing key to help breed some confidence. Nick Faldo and David Leadbetter have been a very good marriage, and this is not a slam on David, but everyone thinks they now need to have a method with their golf swing in order to become some sort of valuable golfer. That's hogwash! All you need to do is shoot a low score to be a valuable golfer and your swing can take any shape or form. You don't have to have a teacher with you. You don't have to be working on a certain method!

'In fact, I'm not so worried about all this at the top level of the game – they are all grown men and can do as they please. But I am a little worried about the influence it may be having at the grass roots. It's a little disturbing that people might think they have to work at a particular swing form or shape and practise in a certain manner in order to be able to go out and enjoy their golf. I just don't buy that. In terms of Nick and David, it's just fashionable.

'There is no question that many people are convinced that they can do what Faldo did – rebuild a swing – and then win with it. They should be a little more realistic and look at other people who have tried that and not succeeded. In fact ruined their careers. Back in the thirties, Ralph Guldhal, who was an outstanding player, winning US Opens back to back, and a Masters title, wrote a book about his golf swing and having analyzed it, could never play again. He simply could not play any more. There have been others. Bill Rogers was a great natural talent who tried to change some things, and has never been heard of since. Sandy Lyle, a great golfer – absolutely absurd that he should have changed his entire mechanics, the entire shape of his golf swing. I mean your brain, muscles, attachments are pretty well blueprinted by the time you are twenty years old and to try to remap that whole thing, well, it ain't gonna work in a lot of cases. So you look at Faldo and you say, "Hey, great going, you've done a marvellous job. You should be commended for your discipline, your dedication. Hats off to your coach." Is that for everybody? I don't think so.

'The record of Jack Nicklaus is phenomenal, the best in history. Yet if you ask people about his golf swing, they dismiss it entirely, and they say that his successes were due to his mental talents, his unbelievable ability to concentrate and focus and prepare himself mentally. Those were his keys to success, and his golf swing is dismissed. I don't know how you can do that, but it has been done. Ben Hogan on the other hand – his swing is considered by many to be a blueprint for everyone's golf swing.

Hogan winning his third major of 1953, the Open at Carnoustie. No player has won as many in a year since the War.

Byron Nelson had a great record, but no one talked of his golf swing. So its completely individual and subjective. It's just up to the writers and the players of the time as to whose golf swing becomes a model and whose doesn't.'

The perfect swing remains a holy grail, in the quest for which modern players have attending them at major championships, the teaching guru, the physiotherapist and the psychologist. One of them doesn't. He is Lee Trevino, who says, 'The only reason I don't have a guru is that I can't find one good enough to beat me.'

The Caddies

The word 'caddie' derives, as do so many other words in Scottish usage, from the French. The French word 'cadet' is used in the sense of 'younger' as in a younger brother, or even the youngest brother, in a family. It could also mean a porter. The early caddies were essentially club carriers expected to tend the flagstick, tee-up the master's ball on a little mound of sand which they would build, and essentially keep quiet. In time, clubs were carried by anyone with an interest in the game and an interest in earning a few shillings. And at such places as

The **'gypsy' caddies** in 1946, so different to the 'shot consultants' of today.

St Andrews, Musselburgh and North Berwick, caddies would be drawn from club- or ball-makers with time to spare, the unemployed, and it has to be said, local layabouts.

As the game and the courses developed, caddies became willy-nilly advisers and confidantes, particularly if their masters were engaged in money matches. Many of them were capable players of the game, almost all of them cryptic commentators on the playing techniques of their employers. Always there was a certain gypsy flavour about them persisting through the twenties and thirties and further as the numbers of professional events increased and the tournament players could begin to think of having regular, travelling caddies. The caddies then would materialize at distant venues, hitch-hiking on the roads, or dodging ticket collectors on trains. They seemed to come in all shapes and sizes, and all ages. When Daniels, who worked the courses at Deal and Sandwich, carried the bag for Gene Sarazen, Open Championship winner at Princes in 1932, he was all of 65 years old.

Max Faulkner, not surprisingly, had the knack of attracting very distinctive caddies. He said,

'I had a very good caddie, Tom Turner from Sunningdale. He was a shunter on the railway, a member of Sunningdale Artisans and pretty much a scratch player. A big, good-looking fellow. He had a bet with someone that he'd let his hair and his beard grow for a year. You can imagine what he looked like after six months. He caddied for me in lots of tournament locally, but he came to an Open at Lytham and as we were playing the 14th, I'll never forget it, half a dozen women came running up the side of the fairway, screaming. I had all my colours on and I thought blimey, they're after me. But they never looked at me. It was Tom they were after, saying to each other, "That's him, that's him." I choked him off, and told him he'd better get that beard off.

'Mad Mac was with me for a long time – a wonderful pianist he was. Once we were in Ireland and I took Dai Rees and Ken Bousfield down to this pub in Bray, where Mac was playing – top of the piano off, and so on. Must have been 100 people in the place. There were half a dozen other caddies in the room, and they passed hats round, making a collection for the pianist. People put two bob in, I put two bob in. I thought it was all for Mac, 'cause he didn't drink. He was like me, never touched it while a tournament was on. But when he had finished playing, all the other caddies had vanished up the road with the money, and boozed it away in another pub!

'He got the name Mad Mac because he used to go off, go a bit silly, once a year. I'd say, "Look here, Mac, you've got to go inside for a bit, things are not right." He used to get stupid. And he'd go in and have a bit of treatment and come out, right as rain for a while. Lovely fellow. Going up north, I'd say, "I'll pick you up somewhere on the A1, about a hundred miles up, but you'd better be at the side of the road." There was a bit of dual carriageway near Stamford in those days. Mac had an old cleek – thick grip, wooden shaft – a lovely, powerful club. I came across him punching iron shots up the main road with this club. I pulled up – "Hello Mac." "Hello Mr Faulkner." It was always Mr Faulkner. That was discipline. He had been in the Royal Flying Corps in the first war, you see. I said, "great." And jumped out, and hit half a dozen shots up the road. Not many cars about then, even on a main road. Then we jumped in the car, drove on, and tried to find them.

'He used to have an ancient anorak with a big square patch on the back on which he'd chalk tips for the horses. When I won the Dunlop Tournament in 1946, I played with Charlie Whitcombe on the last day. We started down the first hole at Southport, that short hole, with maybe 150 people. As we drove off down the second, we thought, "What have we done?" All these people were running back to the clubhouse to place bets on Mac's tips. They caught up with us at the fourth.'

Mad Mac was probably all but the last of a dying breed: the wanderers, the gypsies who'd sleep in a bunker, in an old shed, under a tractor. They would come out like the great unwashed, drinking too much, and on the move all summer. Then spend the winters in search of warm, urban places. These characters persisted through much of the fifties, but they were not able to cope with the rise and rise of tournament golf in the public esteem and they simply melted away. Increasingly, tournament sponsors, ever mindful of the exposing eye of the television camera, put caddies into uniform. And as the financial rewards increased, so caddies became more aware of their responsibilities as semi-public figures.

Willie Aitchison, a Glasgow man based for many years in Southport, was one of the great reformers in this respect. He caddied for

Roberto de Vicenzo, the Argentine player, when he won the Open Championship at Hoylake in 1967. He caddied for Lee Trevino in his victories at Birkdale in 1971, Muirfield in 1972 and at all of Trevino's appearances in the UK subsequently. As proud as any Scot, Aitchison was often incensed at his fellow caddies' behaviour and appearance, and never hesitated to tell them so. He had an acute awareness of what victory in these great championships meant to professional golfers, his clients, and paid an almost finicky attention to the details and responsibilities of his work.

The style of Mad Mac and his anorak was not the style of Willie Aitchison, nor for that matter of David Musgrove, who caddied at home and abroad for Sandy Lyle for many seasons. Nor of Peter Coleman, who served Bernhard Langer in the same way. Thus by the eighties, the caddie was a completely different animal and with the approval of the PGA European Tour, they were able to form their own association, reflecting their place in the enormous growth worldwide of the old game and the attractive image it was able to present on the world's television screens.

With all this came very substantial rewards. The caddie of any one of the game's top half dozen superstars might well earn $100 000 in a year, and travel the world in some style. On the other hand Philip Mobley, known as Pete or more often 'Wobbly', who caddies for Ian Woosnam, spends 'about £20 000' on flights and travel and accommodation in the course of a year. Woosnam of course is a completely international player, and in the course of any one year will make one trip to Australia, one to Japan, and two or more to the USA, on top of his routine UK and Europe travelling. Life with Woosnam is the top of the trade. Philip started much nearer the bottom. He said:

'I started with a fellow called David Jagger from Selby Golf club, I think with something like £10 a round. Just like an apprenticeship, really. I was a junior member at Selby, and got to the stage when I was going there every day practising and playing, with ambitions in the game. But I realized that I was never going to be good enough, and when David offered me the chance to start caddying, I thought it would be a good chance to see a bit of Europe, and a good chance to grow in a sense as well.

'I used to stay with David wherever he stayed, and he'd drive me to tournaments, so it was easy in that respect. There was not a lot of money involved – soon after I started with David, indeed when I finished with David, I was finding it a struggle. I didn't have much money in the bank, and I'd have to live in bed and breakfasts. To get to tournaments meant the train, and that could mean two and three days' journey to Italy, for example. And I've stayed in some flea pits – shower on one floor, room on the other, and you needed a key to get into the shower. Some experience! Still, I learned, and moved on with other players – Gordon Brand Jr, Ian Baker-Finch in the Open of 1984, which taught me a lot, and Howard Clark before Ian.

'I suppose I am at the pinnacle of my career now. That Open with Baker-Finch was very important. I really learned then what the pressure is when you go into the last round on an Open leading the championship. I was only 20 years old then. The pressure on every shot is intense, and having experienced that has helped me a lot with Ian Woosnam. He has been in that situation quite a few times. On these days, the trick is to calm your man down, keep him cool. I talk to him a lot, try to keep his concentration going, and boost him along. At the Masters when he took six going down the 13th when after nine we had been cruising, and then he was only one shot ahead, I said to him, "Look, we're still leading this tournament, we're not losing it, you go on and win. We're a shot ahead, not a shot behind". So he went on and did it, won it. But it was a very nerveracking experience. All the time I was thinking that if I made one mistake I might lose him the tournament. So I was trying to concentrate myself, trying to block everything out, just walking down the fairway with a kind of tunnel vision. One bad putt, one missed green could cost him the tournament. But after that 13th hole, he played very solidly.

'If we are playing a major practice round, perhaps on a course he hasn't played before, we'd get to the course about nine. Then Ian would hit a few chips and a few balls just to warm up, then to the first tee. He likes to know the driving lines from the tees, except on the par three holes, of course. So I try to give him these – where to hit it, which side of the fairway to place it and so on, until he gets to know the course. I clean the clubs every day, wiping the grips, making sure we have enough balls in the bag, and just making the basic checks of the equipment.

'If he needs me to look at his swing, if he thinks there is something wrong which I might spot, he'll ask me, but at the major events he has Bob Torrance with him to check that. So basically it is just getting everything in order so that on the first tee I hand him a glove and a ball. He knows there are not more than 14 clubs in the bag, and he can be relaxed and not jumping about. If he loses interest, or gets a little bored on a practice round, I'll have a bet with him, give him odds on making a birdie at the next hole, just to keep him going. On practice days, it is relaxed and steady and you just try to take it all in. But once the gun goes off I try to give it 110 per cent just by talking to him, and no-body else, and try to get on with the business. We get along like brothers in a way. I think Ian feels that I'll do a good job for him, that I want him to do well all the time, which is nice.

'Different players have different attitudes. Some like to say when they've finished for the day "see you tomorrow" and that's that. I go down to Ian's house for Christmas, sometimes for the week and play a little golf, a couple of times a year. Some players expect you to be right all the time, and they never say good club or anything. Often caddies don't get the reward for doing a good job. But things have changed a lot. The Caddies Association formed in the mid-eighties means that we now have some facili-ties, where we can sit down after a round, or get out of the rain. We are welcome in most clubhouses now, which doesn't mean we have to go in, but it's good to know that we can.

'Being with a player like Ian Woosnam, I get some perks. Ian plays Maruman clubs, and they look after me to a degree. Fanny's got a few endorsements through Nick. People are looking to put names on you, so you'll advertise their product. Usually when we go to tournaments abroad, I stay with Ian. But now I can afford to stop where I want, in good hotels, because when Ian is earning money, I am earning money. Now I can afford my own car, for instance, which some caddies can't. I have a basic wage, plus $7\frac{1}{2}$ per cent of Ian's prize money, which is a nice little turnover. You have to give and take. At the US Open when he finished second, he had two cards on which he had run out of credit. We had to get back in a hurry. The only way was Concord, and to get to Concord we had to hire a private plane. I had a credit card that worked. We got back, and he paid me back! Now that he has won his first major, his one big ambition is to win the British Open.'

Wobbly and **Woosie** – a great team.

Perhaps the ultimate emancipation of the caddie is the fact that we now have a 'lady caddie' at the top of the game in the person of Fanny Sunesson, a Swedish girl who has caddied for Nick Faldo, and one or two other ladies on the circuit. Fanny rather drifted into the caddie business. She played a good deal of amateur golf in Sweden, and to quite a high standard. She wanted to see how the professionals did it, from inside the ropes, so she caddied in the 1986 Scandinavian Masters, and at another tournament in Sweden. Someone suggested that she should become a regular caddie, and should give it a trial, for a month. She did.

'I thought it would be a nice way to travel and be involved with golf. I started learning how to do the yardages. Someone had to tell me to do it! But you learn things all the time. My first serious bag was Jose Rivero, for almost the whole season of 1987. I had a friend, she caddied as well. They all looked after me – the fellows were really nice to me, helped me with places to stay and where to go, and everything. They didn't give me a hard time, or anything like that. Apart from the fact that I couldn't go to the toilet as easily as they could, there was nothing.

'I clean all the grips on Nick's clubs every morning and dry them off, and check the supply of balls and the equipment generally. I always look at his swing and if I see anything, I would tell him. Sometimes I can't see anything, I'm not that good really. And if David Leadbetter, his coach is there, well, I just listen, and take it all in. With Nick, there have been a lot of changes in my life. I've travelled more. I'm more well known now. People recognize me more which is nice sometimes and hard work sometimes. I suppose I get more time off, but the weeks I work are more intense. And being at these bigger tournaments is very thrilling.'

Fanny Sunesson, a good golfer in her own right and fully qualified to have one of the top 'bags' of the game.

CHAPTER FIVE

SHARPENING THE TOOLS OF THE TRADE

In the past 20 years, there have been remarkable changes in the 'accoutrements' of the game, in clubs, balls, greenkeeping equipment and machinery, pesticides, fertilizers, everything. Whether it is cause and effect, chicken or egg, I know not, but there is also a huge increase in the number of people playing golf, at least 40 million worldwide it is suggested. And the golf trade, servicing these people, has now become a very substantial industry. Thus in the bigger professionals' shops, in the city centre retail outlets, and even through mail order, the unsuspecting club golfer endures a barrage of enticements for wound balls, two-piece balls with balata or Surlyn covers, and clubs featuring radial soles, cavity-backed heads, peripheral weightings, graphite shafts, titanium shafts, boron shafts and carbon fibre this that and t'other.

Changes, we have to believe, mean improvements and nowhere has this been more pronounced than in the golf ball. The wound ball, in principle the Haskell ball, dates from the turn of the century. Coburn Haskell, a Cleveland golfer, was visiting the Goodrich Rubber Company factory at Akron in Ohio when he saw some thin rubber strips lying as waste material. He had the notion that by winding these threads round a rubber core, he might have a very lively golf ball. He went to work on his idea with the help of Bertram Work, a Goodrich engineer, and by the turn of the century, had his ball. When Walter Travis won the US Amateur Championship of 1901 with the ball, and Sandy Herd won the Open Championship of 1902 playing with Haskells, the gutty was consigned to history. The new ball was livelier. It went further, could be mishit and yet give an acceptable result, unlike the perfect hit which the gutty required. The Haskell was easier to get into the air. It zipped off an iron club and altogether was much more encouraging to beginner golfers.

It has three components in core, rubber thread winding, and

cover. The two-piece ball dispenses with the rubber winding, and simply has a larger rubber core with a cover. These covers are made of balata or of Surlyn, a synthetic material produced by the Du Pont Company. It seems almost impossible to 'hack' these modern balls – cut right into the cover – as a bad mishit with an iron club would do quite easily to the earlier balls. Even more important is the fact that modern balls, because of quality control in manufacture, are about as uniform as they can be. In the old days, in every dozen balls, there would be a few which quite frankly were not very good. Not so today. Lee Trevino is a fan of the two-piece ball. He calls it, 'the greatest, biggest technology of all. A guy now, instead of cutting it up, can play three or four rounds with it. You cannot knock that ball out of shape. Now a wound ball, I don't care who makes it, once you've hit that ball once, it's not round any more. It cannot be. . . .'

Such are the skills of the manufacturers today, in the use of materials and in the pattern of the dimples on the cover, that golf balls can be made with particular flight characteristics built into them. In

Above:
The Haskell ball – one of the great revolutions in golf.

Below:
The three-piece wound ball still in its mould.

the words of Johnny Miller:

'Now they have dimple patterns that have so much lift and do so many correcting things to a golf ball ... they can take the spin off a golf ball, and use a harder cover that is more responsive to get more distance. You can almost find a ball, like it was dial-a-ball, that suits your game. And I think it's the ball that is the secret to the game.'

Many of the leading personalities in the professional game are concerned about trends which they see as taking much of the finesse out of the game. Tony Jacklin says,

'I still like to think that you have to play shots in golf: that you have to have little fades, little pushes, little draws and little hooks and make it all work that way. A lot of guys coming into the game now don't know any shot but stand over the ball and bust it. And they just hit that one shot all the time. And the equipment ... leans towards that, becoming ... the way to play the game.'

Greg Norman is even more vehement on the subject of technology and its effects on the game.

'I think technology has ruined the top player. Now that's a pretty strong statement that I made there, but I think technology has come along so quickly in the last three or four years that it is taking away shotmaking. It has taken away the better player's ability to manoeuvre the golf ball and put his mind onto the clubface and make that ball do whatever he wants it to do ... a golf ball doesn't curve nearly as much as it did in 1983 or 1982. You can't work a golf ball – put a soft curve or a soft fade on it. You can't do that nowadays because the aerodynamics of a golf ball are getting so good that a ball now kind of corrects itself. If it's on a slicing path it will now correct itself and go straight towards the hole. That's great for 98 per cent of golfers in the world, 'cause they're the ones that need help and get enjoyment out of the game. But for the better players, it's actually a detriment, because I know I like to be able to work the ball. I know I like to be able to hit a flyer every now and then when I need to hit it. I like to be able to execute a shot when I need to hit it, and it's very difficult with the equipment you've got.'

Frank Thomas is technical director at the US Golf Association, and as such, is probably much closer to the situation than even a senior tour player like Greg Norman.

'In the beginning it was an art: go out and get a stick and fashion a club. Now we have applied modern materials to equipment, and I see equipment as now being under control. The balls have reached the maximum as far as the distance they can go and I see a bright future for the game. Very bright. You can be too restrictive with specifications for the ball, for example, and if we had been rigid, we would still have had the gutta percha ball and the hickory shaft. I don't think the game would be where it is today. But look at the performances of some of the people who had the, shall we say old, equipment, such as Bob Jones. Look at the performance record Byron Nelson has and Hogan and Nicklaus. People aren't performing that way today. The game has progressed over a long period of time. Now I think people believe what they read. I think, in many cases, equipment has been hyped out of proportion, but that is part of the game, of the mystique of the game. If you really believe it is going to do it for you, it probably will! I don't know how you define confidence but people perform well when they have confidence in their equipment.

'Back in 1963, Jack Nicklaus won a long-drive contest with a hit of 341 yards. It is more the people than the equipment which is giving us any increased distances we may be seeing. When somebody says that a piece of equipment is hitting the ball 20–30 yards further, I am extremely sceptical. We've done some tests on balls that were produced in the 60s and we find that the differences are in the neighbourhood of about ten yards as compared to the ball of today. The difference is about eight yards in the carry area and ten yards in the overall distance. As I said, in 1963 Jack Nicklaus was driving the ball tremendous distances.

'Do you know, we test over 850 balls on the conforming ball list. Of the top 100 balls there are only ten yards' difference from the maximum distance to ball number 100. I don't believe that if you shortened the ball by 30 yards say, that you would break up that bunching. In every athletic activity that we are involved in today, people are getting better and better and better, and the difference between the extraordinary and the common place is shrinking, in every activity. Why should golf be different?

'When you talk of the spin characteristics of a ball, basically that has to do with the cover material. Now you're getting soft-covered two-piece balls that spin tremendously. But you get

'Iron Byron', the manufacturers' golf ball tester – it's yet to hit a bad shot!

nothing for free. A ball that has a high spin rate will usually surrender some length. Somewhere along the line you have to give something up. There is very little magic involved. We are now spending $1.5 million on more research programmes, mathematically modelling every aspect of the game, and we believe we are going to be able to quantify in scientific terms every part of the game. And for the sole purpose of making sure that technology does not substitute for skill.

'There is a mystique about this game. The game is so mental that you can take a golf ball, and if you don't believe that golf ball is the right one for you, you will not hit a good shot with it. If you are used to a particular brand of golf ball, and pick up another ball which is exactly the same, something in your mind will say, "This is not right, I'm not going to hit this well." It happens to every golfer. And you can't have different rules for different people. I can hit the ball like Greg Norman. But I can do it only once in a round, and when I do it, I feel so excited about it, and I can say I hit it just like Norman. That's the relationship the average guy has with the super professionals and if you break that relationship, you've had a tremendous effect on the game. I can't relate to the top professionals if they are using a different product. I don't see anything out there to worry us. The game is very healthy, and that should be the concern of the USGA.'

One man who is at the sharp end of all this is Wally Uihlein of the Acushnet Company, makers of Titleist golf balls. He believes that technology makes the game's traditions.

'Is golf a game, is golf an art, is golf a science? I think it is a combination of all three and I think technology has been the greatest democratizing force in the history of golf. If it were not for technology, the game would not be as affordable, and played by as many people as enjoy the game today. Technology made clubs and balls more affordable, because of economies of scale in production and the use of contemporary materials. But technology is associated with change and change, by its very nature, involves risk. Particularly in a game of deep rooted traditions; in rules, architecture, equipment, and skills.

'This game is a combination of the player, the club and the ball. It involves competition with oneself, with one's fellow man and with the course. In understanding the golf shot, we are not really talking about "Does the ball go too far?" Not until the publication of *The Search for the Perfect Swing* by Cochrane and Stobbs in the sixties did we have a better understanding of the golf swing. The ball is what travels. So in many cases when you feel that you are hitting the ball further, the assumption is that it is the quality of the ball that matters, because the ball travels. But it may be changes in your swing to bring about a more effective "launch condition". Or there may have been some changes in the club that you used. The ball, the club and the golfer coinciding produces this force-transfer condition which produces the golf shot. And again, it is the ball which is focussed on because it is the component which travels.

'Yes, today's ball is different. It's different by virtue of its construction and by virtue of the materials which go in it. One of the great changes which affected the worldwide golf ball industry was the universal acceptance of the 1.68"-diameter ball in the late 1970s. Until then, US manufacturers were making that size ball and the rest of the world was making a smaller ball. There was limited competition, restricting the process of making the product better. Then suddenly for the five leading ball manufacturers (of whom two, incidentally, are in Japan), you had the forces of competition focussing on one product, one set of specifications.

'The golf ball today is better than it was ten years ago. And that one was better than ten years before that. It is more consistent. It is longer. It is longer because we understand more about the forces that produce distance. That's a by-product of aerospace exploration. The fact is that jets today are more efficiently designed. The Concord is a more efficient airplane than the DC-9 of the fifties. That's a result of what we've learned about objects in motion over the last 30 years. This information is as much applicable to golf balls in flight as it is to airplanes in flight.

'A lot of what we learned about golf balls in flight, and putting them into flight, was a by-product and fall-out from the space race. Before 1955 there were very few academic programmes looking at that phenomenon. The whole space competition between the USA and the then Soviet Union led to an increase in the number of academic programmes that addressed these phenomena. All other industries benefited from it. There is no question in our minds that we learned from working with the Massachussetts Institute of Technology on a lot of fundamentals which they had established through their involvement in the space programmes. And we applied that learning to making golf balls fly better, fly straighter, fly longer.

'There are six major forces that strike at the heart of the debate between technology and tradition. The first two are golf ball-related. The first is the fact that golf balls today are better, more consistent, with the use of contemporary materials and the processes that technology has evolved. Second is the working knowledge that we have of the aerodynamic forces at work. We know much more than we did 10, 20, 30 years ago. The third variable is the golf club. Today, they too are more efficiently designed. The weight distribution is more effective, not only making the ball go further, but also go straighter.

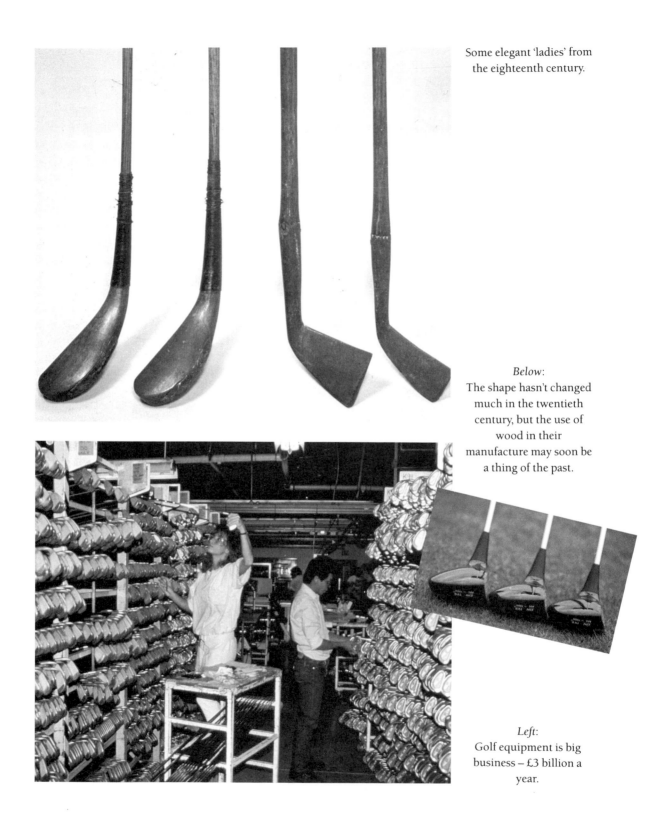

Some elegant 'ladies' from the eighteenth century.

Below:
The shape hasn't changed much in the twentieth century, but the use of wood in their manufacture may soon be a thing of the past.

Left:
Golf equipment is big business – £3 billion a year.

'A fourth variable, and I think it is a very important one, is the role and involvement of what I call "swing doctors". The fact is that week in, week out, on the PGA Tour, on the Volvo European Tour, you have David Leadbetter, Peter Kostis, Bob Torrance and others on site, to instruct and aid the world's finest players.

'Fifth, and I think this is an important one, let's look at today's great players: Ian Baker–Finch is 6'4" and 195 pounds; Steve Elkington is 6'2" and 190 pounds and Davis Love is 6'3", compared to Tom Watson at 5'9" and 160 pounds, Tom Kite at 5'7" and 155 pounds, and Jack Nicklaus at 5'11" and 190 pounds. That is going to allow these fellows to strike the ball rather differently.

'The sixth component, and it is a very important one, is golf course architecture and maintenance. These players are playing on courses that are better conditioned, that have fairways that are carpet-like, with greens that are soft and receptive to the ball in much more user-friendly ways than courses in the old days when they were designed to be hard and fast and put a premium on control round the greens.

'So you have six variables. Three are product, two of them are player-related, one of them is facility-related. They all interact to make possible a game which is entirely different to the one we knew 30, 40 or 50 years ago.

'You may mention Ian Woosnam and Corey Pavin as small guys who generate distance. Agreed. But we are suggesting that players, as in all sports, are bigger, stronger, and in better condition.

'The players on the Senior Tour, generally feel they are hitting the ball so much further, and they attribute that to the golf ball. One of the first things to do is look at the equipment they use. The fact is that Senior players today are not using the same clubs they used 20 years ago. So you've got a change in the club, a change in the ball, and you've got a change in the condition of the courses they are playing. It's the total – they have greater distance generating capabilities today than they had 20 years ago.

'There's no question that when you take the club of today with the ball of today, you've got a one plus one equals three phenomenon. It is very difficult to make absolute statements because you can't leave out that third component, the golfer.

'The golfer brings to the golf shot a set of basic launch conditions: his angle of attack and his clubhead speed. And these have to be taken into consideration before you can make any statement as to how far the ball is going to travel, and what might be the role of the club. Seve Ballesteros has the idea that it might be sensible if in the majors, everyone played with the same equipment, but I think that is a dangerous consideration, and I'll explain why.

'Let's say that the ball declared for the championship is a high-spin ball, one with high spin characteristics. Mark O'Meara's "launch conditions" favour a higher spinning golf ball. He is a medium spin player. Payne Stewart's launch conditions have a very steep angle of attack. He puts a lot of spin on the ball naturally, so he wants a lower-spinning ball. That's why the suggestion is dangerous – I would not want to be the man who decided which ball specifications were to be adopted.

'There is no question that the adoption of a narrower range of specifications, whether in golf ball or golf club, would force players to make adaptations and changes to their swing, so that they would optimize it as it relates to these fixed set of specifications, whether for ball or club. And again, this game is played by people who range from 5'4" and 130 pounds to 6'7" and 225 pounds. So it would be very difficult to define a set of specs right in the middle, and fair to everyone. Frankly, it would not be good for the game. It would lead to a higher level of discouragement, at both competitive level and everyday level, and I can't see how that is in the best interest of perpetuating the game we all enjoy.

'The USGA and the R & A specifications are examples of the relationship between the game and technology really being a partnership and not an adversarial one. The fact is that for over 50 years there have been governors of the weight, size and velocity of the golf ball, and in the last ten years there have been additional statutes. One was the overall distance standard, then later the symmetry rule – the insurance that balls would have to perform symmetrically if they were to receive USGA and R & A conformance adoption. These are examples of where the manufacturers work cooperatively with the institutional forces in the game. So I reinforce the fact that, since the product is shipped voluntarily in conformity with the rules of the game, the relationship is a partnership, not adversarial. But it needs to be a participation process, not an exclusive one.'

FOUR HOLY
GRAILS

·

In world golf, four championships are considered of the highest importance. They are in order of play each year the Augusta Masters (USA) in April, the US Open Championship in June, the Open Championships (Britain) in July and the US PGA Championship, played in August. They are generally known as the 'majors', and all four are known collectively as the 'Grand Slam'. Only four golfers have won all four championships. They are Gene Sarazen, Ben Hogan, Gary Player and Jack Nicklaus.

The origin of the expression 'Grand Slam' is from bridge, of course, but in golf it was used originally to describe the staggering achievement of Robert Tyre Jones Jr – 'Bobby' Jones – in 1930, when he won the amateur championships of both Britain and America and the Open championships of both countries.

In the decade of the twenties, he won the US Amateur Championship five times, the US Open four times, the Open Championship three times, the British Amateur Championship once. He played six times in Walker Cup competition, and won every match he played.

Jones' father was a prosperous attorney in Atlanta. He was a sickly child, and his father, a member of the Atlanta Athletic Club, would take a summer cottage out by the club's golf course at East Lake on the edge of the city, to give the boy some country air. By the time he was seven, the boy was pottering around the course. In 1913, at the age of 11, he read about the US Open in which Francis Ouimet had beaten Vardon and Ray, and in the same year, saw the two great English players play an exhibition in Atlanta. Bobby Jones was a golfer. Before the year was out, he had scored 80 round the East Lake course.

He played in the American Amateur Championship before his fifteen birthday and got through two rounds at Merion before losing to the experienced Bob Gardner, who was a finalist that year. Jones was a prodigy. He played very little golf in the winter during his college

Bobby Jones with his
unique haul of 1930.

days which embraced Georgia College of Technology for mechanical engineering, Harvard for an English degree, then Emory College, where he qualified as a lawyer. Yet through the decade of the twenties, while still in his twenties and amidst generations of outstanding professionals, he dominated the US Open as Hagen was dominating the British Open. Jones won in 1923, 1926, 1929 and 1930. At the same time, he all but overwhelmed the US Amateur, winning five times in the eight years from 1923 to 1930 when he retired.

It is generally accepted that the Grand Slam of Jones, the amateur from Atlanta, Georgia, can never be duplicated. The power and depth of the modern professional game is such that the amateur championships of both nations are now much less important from a media and public interest point of view, with talented amateurs now turning professional when scarcely out of their teens.

The Augusta Masters did not exist in 1930. Indeed it was Jones in his retirement who created the Augusta National course. In 1934, Jones inaugurated an invitational tournament which from a quite modest beginning, developed into the now world-famous Masters.

The ultimate Grand Slam would be for a golfer to win, in one year, all four of the majors, all of them professional events. The closest anyone has come to this was when in 1953, Ben Hogan won the Masters, the US Open and the British Open, but could not compete in the US PGA. There was simply not time for him to get from Carnoustie to Birmingham, Michigan, near Detroit, to prepare for the US PGA event.

For professional golfers the majors are *the* tournaments to win and guarantee an instant place in the golfers' Hall of Fame. Winning for the first time can take some getting used to as Lee Trevino remembers:

'When I first won a major, I didn't feel that I was playing with history. I didn't know Ben Hogan existed. I was playing golf, and didn't know the man existed. Talk about Byron Nelson and Sarazen and Jones and his record – when I came up, we were trying to figure out where the next meal would come from, you understand what I am saying? I tell people this and they say "You must be joking – you didn't know who Hogan was?" Believe me, I was 20-something years old before I realized there was a Jones and a Hagen and a Nelson and a Sarazen, and you name them, and a Mangrum and a Hogan. I lived in Dallas. I had no idea. We didn't watch television, we didn't have electricity. How the hell could we watch television? We didn't, my grandfather listened

Any time you win a major championship, it is just a level above all the other tournaments you play. That's what is important. That's what makes it special.

Tom Watson

— 94 —

to baseball on a battery radio. The only time we could turn the radio on was when the Dallas Eagles played. So no, I never knew anything about it, nothing.

'I didn't really think I belonged, from the beginning. Coming from the caddie ranks, and playing with guys like Arnold Palmer and Jack Nicklaus, and who have you. I won the US Open at Rochester and was scared to death. Even though I won the golf tournament I was scared to death. I didn't know what I was going to say at the press conference – didn't know because I was fresh – didn't know anything. When I won the Hawaiian Open later, in October, that settled me more. But the thing that gave me most confidence of all was when I won the US Open in 1971. That gave me comfort, because I felt like, hey, you do belong here.'

The Open Championship

The Open Championship dates from 1860, and for that reason alone, some would say it is the greatest of all golf tournaments. It grew from the creation of the Prestwick club in 1851, and from the energies and vision of one James Ogilvy Fairlie of Coodham, a property some five miles from Prestwick. Fairlie, who had been captain of the R & A in 1850, was a founder member of Prestwick. He was intrigued by the professional game and wrote to a number of clubs, suggesting a medal play event for professionals. None of the other clubs seemed to want to be involved, so Prestwick went ahead in 1860, commissioning a handsome red leather belt from goldsmiths in Edinburgh, at a cost of £25 and announcing that a tournament for professionals only would be played on 16 October.

I think every one of them is important but if I would have to choose one, I would go for the British Open, because it is more open, gives more chances to everybody and it is the oldest tournament. I think it is the tournament that is much more recognized than the other three.

Severiano Ballesteros

Eight players entered and played 36 holes of golf (three rounds of Prestwick's 12 holes course) and the winner of The Belt was Willie Park of Musselburgh. In the following year, the competition admitted amateurs in a field of 12 and was truly an 'Open' championship. James Fairlie played in that Open. For the decade of the sixties, the Open was played at Prestwick and was dominated by Park (three wins), Old Tom Morris (four wins) and Young Tom Morris, whose three successive wins in 1868, 1869 and 1870 meant that the splendid belt became his property.

The championship was in abeyance for a year in which Prestwick arranged with the R & A and the Honourable Company, that it should rotate through their three courses and that they should subscribe for a

new trophy. This was to be the famous 'claret jug' Open Championship trophy. It cost £30, ten pounds more than the total prize fund in 1872. For the next 20 years, the Open was played at Prestwick, St Andrews and Musselburgh, until the Honourable Company moved to Muirfield in 1891. And the period saw the victory of the first Englishman and the first amateur in John Ball of Liverpool, to win in 1890. In 1892, the competition was extended to 72 holes and was promptly won by Harold Hilton also from Hoylake, in the very first of Muirfield's Opens.

Championships are made, ultimately, by champions, and the story of the game of golf time and again throws up a personality dominant in his era. On many occasions, this dominance has been shared, or contested, by two, or even three contemporaries.

In the 21 years from 1894, Harry Vardon won six times, John Henry Taylor five times, James Braid five times: a 'Great Triumvirate' indeed. They were clearly exceptional players. In the twenties, Walter Hagen and Bobby Jones, and America took hold of the championship. Hagen won four times, Jones three and there could have been no greater contrast in personalities.

Where Walter Hagen was a creature of flamboyant wardrobes, *gran turismo* cars and the opulent gesture, Bobby Jones was, at least in

Opposite:
Young Tom Morris and 'the Belt' which he won outright for his three consecutive wins between 1868 and 1870.

Below:
Walter Hagen, very much part of the Scott Fitzgerald world of the 1920s.

his early days, shy to the point of introversion. A modest, conservative, family man. Hagen emerged from a working class background – his father had been a blacksmith in the neighbouring railroad yards – and Jones came from the professional middle classes.

I was interested in one thing: the majors – because I know they live long. You could win a million dollars and that will go. But when you win the US Open or the British Open or the Masters or the PGA, that title goes to your grave.

Gene Sarazen

Hagen was the archetypical American – extrovert, bursting with energy and self-confidence. He was born in Rochester, NY, the only son in a family of four daughters, and took to caddying at the Country Club of Rochester. He became a pretty handy golfer, and when he was but 19, by some fluke became professional at the club. In the famous US Open of 1913, when the amateur Francis Ouimet beat the English 'cracks' in a play-off, Walter, aged 21, finished fourth, behind that famous trio, in his very first attempt at his National Open. Hagen got the taste for it. The next year, at the Midlothian Club near Chicago, he opened with a 68 and walked off with it.

Tall, young, and handsome in a darkly flashy manner, Hagen found a new world opening for him. He found that he loved the competition and the glamour of tournaments, the cheers and the gasps of the galleries, the idolising, the attentions of the ladies. He was invited to endorse products, to play in exhibition matches and tournaments. When the war was over, he won the US Open again in 1919, and in 1920 took his first stab at the Open Championship. At Deal, he was washed away in a huge storm, in one of his rounds scoring 85 with an inward half of 48. He finished fifty-third in a field of 54, thus demonstrating another Hagen characteristic – 'If you're gonna lose, lose big'. He came back the following year, this time finishing sixth, behind Jock Hutchison at St Andrews, and in the same year began a series of victories surely unequalled in the history of golf. He won the US PGA, then a match play championship, beating Jim Barnes in the final, three and two. In 1923, he lost to Gene Sarazen in the final at the 38th hole. In 1924, he began a series of four successive championship victories; a total of 20 consecutive matches. He played in six PGA Championships from 1921 to 1927 and lost only one match in thirty, when Sarazen only just beat him in the 1923 final. On top of that, he won the Open Championship in 1922, 1924, 1928 and 1929.

For a few more years, America continued to dominate the Open Championship: Tommy Armour at Carnoustie in 1931, Sarazen at Prince's in 1932, Densmore Shute at St Andrews in 1933, before the coming of Henry Cotton in 1934 at Royal St George's. Then, as now, the championship followed the tradition of always being played on links courses, in a roster of seven or eight courses, usually balanced between England and Scotland. As the circumstances and growth of the championship demanded, new courses were included, and old courses excluded. Troon came in 1923, Lytham St Annes in 1926, and Carnoustie in 1931, but it went after Tom Watson's win in 1975. The Royal Liverpool course at Hoylake was not considered suitable after 1967, when Roberto de Vicenzo of Argentina won. Turnberry in 1977 became the latest addition to the roster.

Throughout the fifties, two very great players commanded the Open in Bobby Locke of South Africa, and Peter Thomson of Australia, with four and five wins respectively. The coming of the jet aircraft meant that Americans could handle an Open without much more than a week away from home, in contast to Byron Nelson's time prewar, when crossing the ocean by sea took the best part of a week in each direction.

And so came Arnold Palmer and his quest for the Centenary Open in 1960. He said,

'The Open to me was a championship that told the whole world what the game of golf was all about, and thinking back in history to the British Empire and the influence it had on the world, was

Arnold Palmer on his way to victory at the 1962 Open at Troon.

vitally important. Oh, it was even more than I expected. It was exciting. At my first Open, I had the opportunity to take a close friend, my father and my wife and I think that trip probably fulfilled more expectations than any of us had anticipated, even though I didn't win that championship. I finished second [to Kel Nagle of Australia by one shot]. It was the fulfillment of a life's dream, not just for me, but for my father also.'

Arnold's victories in 1961 and 1962 inspired his fellow Americans to follow. They did, with a vengeance.

The championship was to see great champions and great dramas still, with the coming of Nicklaus and his three wins, and Tom Watson with a remarkable five wins, matching the achievements of Peter Thomson, James Braid and J.H. Taylor, but not quite reaching the pinnacle of Harry Vardon. The most international of all the four majors, it at last saw a flowering of British and European players taking command in the eighties – Severiano Ballesteros, Sandy Lyle, Nick Faldo. Thus in its long history, the Open has been won by golfers from England, Scotland, Ireland, France, Spain, the United States, Argentina, South Africa, Australia and New Zealand. And every year they come in their hundreds from every golfing country in the world to what has become an enormous sporting spectacle. The fact that it is played, without exception, on a links course gives it a constant quality which has been a major factor in its standing in the world of golf as the greatest of the majors.

The US Open

The US Open in terms of its location from year to year is very different. The sheer size and scale of the United States, its spread of population, means that the USGA which controls the championship is obliged to move the event from city to city, from region to region of the vast American land mass. In addition, the championship cannot be held in the southern states in mid-summer, since the weather there and then is intolerably hot. So the championship is likely to be held on suburban courses, convenient to major cities such as New York, Boston, Chicago, Philadelphia, Detroit, San Francisco, or Los Angeles. If there is a roster of US courses, for these reasons it is likely to run to 20 or 25 venues, but there are 'regulars' – courses considered to be classic US Open venues, such as the Country Club at Brookline, near Boston; Winged Foot in New York; Merion (Philadelphia); Oak Hill at Rochester; Baltusrol near Newark, New Jersey; Oakmont in Pittsburgh; Oakland Hills near Detroit, the Olympic Club in San Francisco and Pebble Beach on the Monterey Peninsula. No links courses there. Pebble Beach is hard by the Pacific Ocean, but would be better described as a 'cliff top' course. Yet when the USGA in 1986 took their championship to Shinnecock Hills on Long Island, where it had been last played in 1896, the grand old course was in texture about as close to a links as they could get and the championship, won by Raymond Floyd, was an outstanding success.

But US Open courses too have a constant if different quality. They are mostly played on parkland courses, densely tree-lined, with narrow fairways, sophisticated gradings of rough – indeed very severe rough – with a fearsome use of water hazards, and greens protected and defended in an almost intimidating way, with bunkering and collars of rough which often extend right across their entrances. The ultimate requirements on US Open courses are iron nerve, and relentless accuracy of shotmaking. A.W. Tillinghast, designer of such Open courses as Winged Foot and Baltusrol, held that 'a controlled shot to a closely guarded green is the surest test of any man's golf'.

Frank Hannigan, at one time the Executive Director of the USGA, golfing journalist and now commentator with the American Broadcasting Corporation, has his own opinion of the courses used for the US Open:

'US Open set-ups. by the way, have been more or less the same now for more than 40 years. What we think of as the way a US Open course looks, feels, and plays was something that developed after World War II. Great emphasis is always put on accuracy, as distinct from length and power. The fairways become relatively narrow targets, 30–35 yards in width and outside them there tends to be very, very serious and penal rough. It's no accident at all that the great figure in golf then was Ben Hogan. And I often think that the USGA officials built their conditions around the way Ben Hogan played.'

Frank Hannigan, former Executive director of the USGA, and now a commentator for ABC.

The US Open, like the game itself in America at least in the beginnings was a matter for the Scots, or the British immigrant professionals. The first three events were played over 36 holes at founder USGA clubs – Newport in 1895, Shinnecock Hills in 1896, and Charles Blair Macdonald's Chicago Golf Club in 1897. Thereafter, it was played over 72 holes and for the first 20 years, the table of winners was stiff with names like Anderson, Auchterlonie, Ross, and Macleod. In 1911, Johnny McDermott, a fiery spirit from Atlantic City, became the first native born American to win the title. He retained it the following year, and when in 1913, Francis Ouimet, the 19-year-old amateur from Brookline, tied with the English stars Harry Vardon and Ted Ray, and won the playoff, American golf came of age. Seldom again would Americans loosen their hold on their own national trophy.

Ted Ray's win in 1920, when Vardon made his third and last tour of America, saw Vardon leading by five shots with seven holes to play when he was swept away by a gale and a rain storm. Ray, aged 43, beat Vardon, aged 50, by one stroke. Fifty years were to pass before another Englishman, Tony Jacklin, became US Open Champion.

Through the twenties, as we have seen, Bobby Jones was the man to beat. Ben Hogan won four times in the late forties and fifties, as Jones had, and was second twice (Jones had been second four times!). From 1962 to 1980, Jack Nicklaus too won four times and finished second three times. Gary Player became the first 'foreign' player to win in modern times. In 1970, Tony Jacklin's victory, by a stunning seven strokes, was to have momentous consequences for British and European golf. David Graham won for Australia in 1981. Otherwise the American championship belonged to Americans. Nick Faldo got close, losing to Curtis Strange in a play-off in 1988, and when Strange repeated his win in 1989, Ian Woosnam was in second place. Like the British Open, the US Open has become a huge sports promotion, attracting crowds of 150 000 or more for the week, and is also televised worldwide.

The US PGA Championship

The US PGA championship dates from 1916, and was one of the first creations of the newly formed PGA of America. It was originally a match play event, dominated as we have seen in its early years by Walter Hagen. The great names of American golf are on the trophy. Gene Sarazen and Sam Snead won three times, Byron Nelson, Ben Hogan and Gary Player twice each. But rivalling Hagen's five was, perhaps inevitably, Jack Nicklaus.

The championship was changed to medal play in 1958, and after a period in which many felt that it was being played on courses of not quite the right quality, it now selects the toughest courses in the land, prepared for the event in the same testing manner as are US Open courses. It is fair to say that in the past the US PGA has not made it particularly easy for non-American players to compete and as a result it is probably the weakest of the majors. Frank Hannigan agrees with this, saying:

'The PGA Championship when it started in 1916, was unique because it was (a) the championship of the Professional Golfers Association and (b) it was played at match play which gave it a very special flavour, and great things happened.

'Unfortunately, the intercession of big money, and big money equated with television, killed match play because it's very awkward to televise match play. So the PGA Championship, for better or worse, most of us would think worse, switched over to stroke play in the late fifties.

'Now, in my view, it still warrants its being regarded as one of the four premier events in golf, if you will, a major, but it is certainly the fourth of the majors. The least important of the four.

'Part of the problem has to do with timing. It's played in the United States in August where the chances are the weather can be very, very uncomfortable, can be brutal. Brutally warm and hot and humid, and not very suitable environment for good golf. Greens need to be heavily watered to, well, to stay alive and that's part of the problem with the PGA Championship.'

Sam Snead holds similar views to Hannigan:

'Well, they had such bad finalists in the PGA that nobody showed up hardly for the finals. And they figured now, hey, we've got to go to medal play if we're going to make any money. And I wish they would have a tournament of match play. I just loved match play. I like to play head-to-head.'

The Masters

Now we come to the Masters, beyond any doubt one of the major championships, yet lacking one critical element – it is not an open competition – open to the world – as are the US and British Opens. The Masters is an invitational event, presented and organized not by any national association or federation or governing body, but by a private club. The Augusta National Golf Club decides who should play in the Masters, and issues the invitations. The Masters is also unique in another sense: it is played annually on the same course, in Augusta, Georgia, in April, and is the first major of the year. It is also

We got to the 18th green and I'll never forget it. There were about seven or eight ones on the board. I'm colour-blind, and I looked at it and said to my caddie Willie, I said 'Willie, how many ones on that board are red?' and he said 'Just you, boss'. So there I was, leading by two strokes on the last green. Of course I played a good last round. But it was a tournament of patience, because 286 won. That was 1963, my first Masters.

Jack Nicklaus

the youngest of the four, dating from 1934.

When Bobby Jones retired in 1930, having won all four Amateur and Open Championships on either side of the ocean, he had very strong opinions on the design of golf holes and of how a golf course should be laid out. He had after all, in a span of ten years, played the best courses in Britain and America, and he had thought often of creating a course which would incorporate all of his ideas. He often played social winter golf in Augusta, a small town one hundred miles or so from his home in Atlanta, and something of a winter spa in those railroad days. So too did Clifford Roberts, a New York merchant banker and when a local nursery came on the market at Depression prices in 1931 Jones and Roberts snapped up all 365 acres of it. Jones and the course designer Dr Alister Mackenzie got to work on the ground and by late 1933, had laid out a course which was to become one of the most famous in the world.

The club was to be one for men of substance, members who would be invited from all over the country, hence the title Augusta National. They were friends or business acquaintances of Jones, and for that matter Roberts, and men who had a need for winter golf only. The club in fact closes after the tournament in April, and re-opens in November.

The Augusta course is perhaps the last word in American parkland golf. Wide fairways march between towering pines. The greens are vast, at tournament time lightning fast and with daunting slopes. The bunkers are few, no more than 50 in all and most of them clustered round the greens. There is virtually no rough as such on the course. Beneath the pine trees are carpets of cones and pine needles, so that some kind of recovery shot is always possible. No heather or bracken here. The non-playing areas are planted with magnificent flowering shrubs of azalea, flowering cherry, almond and red bud. It is a most beautiful golf course in the spring. The more cynical of its critics hold that the absence of rough is a major shortcoming, and are inclined to dub the Masters as a 'putting contest'. There is of course, rather more to it than that.

The Masters tournament was started in 1934, when Jones simply invited his golfing chums, including the professionals, to play in what was initially the 'Augusta Invitational'. In the beginning, it was something of a jolly for the boys. Jones himself played in a couple of the early events, which rounded out what was then known among the professionals as the 'winter tour', but at that time, there were other tournaments which were much more important to the professionals. The Western Open, in the Chicago area, and the North and South, at Pinehurst, were examples. In fact, the evolution of the Masters as one of the world's major championships is an intriguing mélange of events, personalities, public opinion and the power of the media in the creation of some kind of instant folklore.

In the 1935 event, Gene Sarazen on his final round, holed a spoon shot second on the par five 15th hole for an albatross or 'double eagle'. It helped him tie the tournament with Craig Wood and go on to win the play-off. In retrospect, the shot has taken on the aura of some kind of miracle, and is certainly in place in the Valhalla of golf shots at Augusta. It is true to say that at the time, it was reported routinely. Now in hindsight, thousands are said to have seen it. Sarazen later said, 'there was a gallery of only a handful of people, at a time when the course was not roped off and spectators could roam the fairways.'

The Masters came to life with the arrival of television in the late fifties and Arnold Palmer. Television, and in particular the further development of colour television, Palmer, and the fact that President Eisenhower, coincidentally, was a keen golfer brought the game to the American public like nothing had since the days of Bobby Jones, and his 1930 Grand Slam.

The outstanding champion of the day was Ben Hogan. Austere, and seemingly remote his play was forbidding perfection, beyond the range of mortals. Palmer, his successor, could not have made a greater contrast. Arnold was the Common Man. His shirt tail hung out. He dragged deeply on cigarettes. He hitched up his pants, and he played the game like a cavalier, but his victories were breathtaking.

In 1960, he birdied the 71st and 72nd holes to win. In the US Open of the same year, he was seven strokes behind going into the last round, with 12 players ahead of him. He birdied the first four holes on the round, took 30 for the front nine, and went round in 65 to win the Open. In the Masters of 1962, he made birdies on two of the last three holes to tie with Gary Player and Dow Finsterwald. In the play-off he was three behind Player with nine holes to play. He played them in 31 strokes and won.

His failures were no less dramatic. In the 1961 Masters, a par four at the last hole would have beaten Gary Player. Palmer bunkered his approach shot, hit the recovery over the green, chipped poorly and took six on the hole. In the 1966 US Open, he squandered a six-shot lead on the last round to Billy Casper, then lost the play off after being

I got a great kick out of Nicklaus. He said something to me that I'll never forget. I wish he'd told me that 20 years ago. He said the easiest tournaments to win of the year are the majors. When he said it I went 'Woo, what are you saying?' Then he said it's because they are the only tournaments the guys are not comfortable with – they come back to you. You just hang in there and make a score, and these guys will fold. If you could learn that early in your career, that would be a great thing to think about.

Johnny Miller

three strokes in front. All this was seen by the vast television audience, slack-jawed, no doubt. He scored ten at one hole in the 1987 Open at Muirfield, when he was going along steadily, having taken five bloody-minded shots in a bunker.

That was Arnold. Much was made of his crackling driving, his majestic long iron play, his zooming approaches. But perhaps his most remarkable talent was in long putting. From 20 or 30 or 40 feet, most players hope to putt up within a couple of feet from the hole. Not Palmer. He expected to hole them, every one of them, and looked offended when he didn't.

And then there was Jones, Bobby Jones, presiding over his twin creations: the course and the competition, receiving the homage of his friends from near and far in his cabin by the tenth tee, and presenting the winner with the club's green jacket, the symbol of triumph in the Masters, at close of play. The tournament was beautifully presented. On-course discipline of the gallery was strict. Food and drink concessions were controlled by the club. There was ample parking. The club was careful never to call this a championship, it has always been a tournament. It initiated a scoreboard service which showed under par scoring in red, and the ten leading players at any one time on huge scoreboards around the course, giving an instant state-of-play at any one time. There is no advertising whatsoever on the property: there were no corporate entertainment facilities and no sponsors. And the players were pampered and protected as nowhere else. Arnold Palmer expressed something of their attitude to the majors and to the Masters in particular:

'The Masters has become worldwide in scope, but in the early days, in my beginning or before that, it was a championship that was known as a US championship. Vitally important to our people but not a worldwide, so to speak, championship. Now I think that it is, a very influential tournament throughout the world, and I think that if any country could pick a championship it would like to have it would be the Masters, because of the atmosphere, the way it's run, the golf course. All the things that are there in Augusta that make the Masters such a great championship.

'I suppose just the drive down Magnolia Lane to the club-house, starts the adrenalin flowing, versus playing in other major championships, where sometimes it becomes a task just to be there and be involved. It isn't a task at Augusta, it's a pleasure, it's

I'm sure some people being introduced to the game now think Tony Jacklin is some old guy that did something in the last century and think of me as I used to think of Vardon and Ray. The fact is I won my two majors only 20 years ago.

Tony Jacklin

Opposite:
Augusta in full bloom. Is there any more beautiful sight in golf?

fun, the golf course is not an ordeal, it's an enjoyment. I think that even the players that go feel like they're at Augusta and they want to win this championship more than any other, but I'm going to do it having fun. And I suppose you look at either of the Open Championships and you think of the deep rough and the challenges and the things you're going to be facing and you know that certainly these are major championships and they're championships you want to win, but at the same time, the sheer enjoyment is not as evident as it is at Augusta.'

Jack Nicklaus, having won the tournament six times, also had feelings about the special qualities of Augusta, but is perhaps more analytical than Palmer:

'Most people consider the Masters the start of the golfing year. Yes, we have some big tournaments, some very good tournaments early in the year, but guys are shadow boxing back and forth, winning tournaments here and there. But to the golfing public, the golfing year really starts with the Masters. We all gear our games to be as sharp as we can come the first part of April.

'I guess I've done it more successfully, the right way, more often than anybody else and what I've done is start thinking about it in January. I used to start preparing in January, the only problem in recent years I don't start preparing until March.

'What I think is special about Augusta is what it means to golf, what Bobby Jones meant to the game of golf. Here's a man who won the four major championships of 1930, he's a man who meant a lot to the game as an amateur, as a leader in the game. He set a lot of direction and people have respected the way he's done things. The courses he's built, the way he's run the golf tournament, the Masters, the way he's put it together. It's just a very special event.

'All I heard about when I was growing up was Bobby Jones, Bobby Jones, Bobby Jones. So I think it was the influence of Jones. He said, when it came to it, you know which the big ones are and they are the ones you must be ready for. That's how I decided I must set out to be ready.

'I won the Amateur in '59 and again in '61. Then when I turned professional, I won the Open in '62, my first year as a professional. Then the Masters in 1963, the PGA the same year, and the British Open not till '66. But it was still pretty early in my career. I was 26 years old, and here I had won all the majors by the time I was 26. In fact I had won four out of five by the time I was 23.'

These then are the major championships. From time to time, other people have claimed that status for other events, the Tournament Players' Championship, for example. Deane Beman has said: 'There are so many good players now that it is difficult for anyone to accumulate a number of individual victories. It could be that it would be good for golf to have five or six majors. It would give individual players more opportunity to excel at these important events.'

Frank Hannigan has his own views on the idea of another major tournament:

'I should think, where there should be a fifth major, if there is going to be such a thing, would be outside the United States. I don't know how to quite make that happen, but I think the reality is that as the game spreads in importance internationally and has more and more good players coming from all over the world, particularly in Asia, that that's where somehow there ought to be a fifth major.'

But the existing, traditional majors are after all the events which carry that certain frisson for the players which perhaps only recent Ryder Cup matches have approached. Certainly Lee Trevino thinks that the majors, as they exist today, are enough: 'I don't think there will ever be another major. It's like the Kentucky Derby. They've got races that race for a lot more money than the Kentucky Derby, but there's only one Kentucky Derby, one Belmont, one Preakness. It's the same with major championships in golf. The media will not stand for it and rightfully so. These tournaments have been there long enough and they've stood through time. If you're going to make everything a major, it don't mean anything.'

Naturally, most of the attention on the majors is focussed on the great success stories, but majors have been lost as often as they have been won. Curtis Strange and Greg Norman are two from recent history who have failed when golf's spotlight was at its brightest.

Curtis Strange of the United States, had his bad times before his good. In the 1985 Masters, with nine holes to play, he was in control of the tournament. On holes numbers 13 and 15, his chance had gone when his ball found water hazards. Subsequent victories in the US Open Championship in 1988 and 1989 allowed him to say that his

Overleaf:
Curtis Strange losing the 1985 Masters. Losses in majors can be very public affairs.

defeat by Langer had not been a 'negative experience':

'No, that was very very positive for me. It was negative from the standpoint that I didn't win, but I learned that it was a terrible feeling to lose a tournament like that and I didn't want to do it again! Not that I wouldn't do it again, but it's something you don't want to experience a lot. I'm not going to say that it helped me in other major championships, but you certainly concentrate harder, which I did in my two other majors. When you come down the stretch, you really concentrate because you certainly don't want to lose again.

'Concentration? You don't get ahead of yourself. You don't think about that trophy, which is so easy to do. You try to think about what you are doing, that this is just a normal golf tournament. And it's not – you've got the most intense pressure in the world on you, maybe for one of the few times in your life. You have to deal with that – go about it like it is normal business, and keep what's at hand uppermost in your mind. Keep this shot, the next shot, the next putt. You can't start wandering – I've done that before and it's cost me dearly!

'To win these big ones, you need experience. You need to be there, be close, a couple of times to see what being in contention really means, learning to deal with the pressure and going ahead and finishing it off. Very few people do that first time. You have to be focussed, plan and play every shot as it comes. Never give up, because they are the toughest to win. There is not only a lot of physical demand, a lot of mental ability is needed too: a lot of inner strength, a lot of guts. These are things you are born with.'

Greg Norman of Australia has had the taste of sweet and sour in major championships. In 1984, he lost a play-off in the US Open to Fuzzy Zoeller. In 1986, he needed a par at the 72nd hole in the Masters to tie the winner, Jack Nicklaus, and didn't get it. In 1987 at the Masters, he lost a play-off against Severiano Ballesteros and Larry Mize, when Mize chipped into the hole from 30 yards for a birdie at the second extra hole.

'When you don't stand up to the pressure, that's golf, that's life. One of my dearest friends is Nigel Mansell, the racing driver, and he and I can relate to that a little bit because it's happened to him in the Grand Prix world and it's happened to me in the golf world. You feel like you have the thing in your grasp, right at the end of your finger tips, then you can't grasp all of it, and it's gone. We are fortunate that we can relate to stuff like that because nobody knows how you feel. You try to be able to express everything but nobody knows how you feel. You try to talk to your wife about it, who's your best friend and confidante. It hurts a lot because you put 199 per cent of yourself into trying to win a golf tournament. But you can't control what other people do, you can't control the mechanic forgetting to put the nut on the wheel so that you can keep going. So you have to be very careful, and accept the fact that you cannot control the destiny of other people. You can only control your own destiny. So to be able to sit there and talk to somebody like Nigel and relate to it, that's a lot easier, because he understands how I feel and I understand how he feels. In the end you both see the light, and decide, well this is the sport I am in.

'And that's the name of the game. . . .'

CHAPTER SEVEN

THE BRIEFCASE
BOYS

·

Mark McCormack,
Chairman of IMG.

International Management Group, or IMG as it is widely known and often feared throughout the world of golf, is the creation of one Mark Hume McCormack, who would probably be described by the more sardonic as a 'Cleveland lawyer'. McCormack might say rather archly that IMG really started with a handshake between himself and Arnold Palmer, who back in 1959, asked Mark to handle his blossoming business. And he will say to this day that he owes everything he has and has achieved to Arnold Palmer.

From the day of the handshake, Palmer's affairs and earning capacities have grown beyond belief, greater now than when he was winning golf's major championships. And McCormack's acumen has driven his IMG to become the biggest and most successful management and promotional company in the world, expanding from golfers and golf-related business to all sports. To the creation of television programmes and negotiating television rights for sports governing bodies, to marketing on behalf of Olympic Games host cities, Papal tours, and the Americas Cup. In its market, IMG is by far the biggest organization. McCormack himself, is a brilliant negotiator and an expert organizer, but also of course a hard-driving employer. Such success has brought him, if not enemies, then critics galore. I asked him to tell me what IMG is, and does. He said:

'To sum up, I suppose it would be a world-wide management service, meaning that golf has become more of an international sport in the last couple of decades than ever before. Jet airplanes take us round the world easily, and you can see in one country televised golf events from another country. That presents a lot of opportunities for the world golfer to earn income from all parts of the world where golf is played, and that too is increasing. So we have offices in something like 19 countries, to take care of the needs of a particular client, whether that client is in the US,

Europe, Japan, Britain, Australia, wherever. Not only his logistical needs when he is playing there, but when he is not . . . trying to market him, his image, his names and his services, to companies and tournaments in that particular country.

'We provide the client with financial management, tax planning, insurance, estate planning, contract negotiations, career guidance. Helping with coaching or technical instruction if required – a very broad base, umbrella service.

'IMG is involved in a lot of elements in golf: there is the managing of players; the creation of special events, some of which become regular established tournaments like the World Match Play or the Dunhill Cup, or the World Championship of Women's Golf. These were all things we conceived and created and have been managing for a long time. Then there is the management of events that other people have created – helping Dunhill run the Dunhill Masters, helping them get players, that sort of thing. We sell television rights to all the major championships: the US Open, the British Open, the PGA and the Masters; producing television for the European PGA Tour where we do the actual production and providing live and highlighted coverage.

Sponsorship is big business: **David Feherty** captaining Ireland's winning team in 1990.

'We have also been involved with the creation and administration of the Sony Rankings, which when all is said and done is the most significant accomplishment I have brought to the game on a global basis, because it was something the sport badly needed and it is something which is becoming more and more recognized and sanctioned as the years have gone on – and I think will become soon just like the tennis rankings. It will be the main criteria by which people are judged.

'I suppose we are involved in publishing. I do a golf annual every year. We do annual editions for many golf tournaments like the British Open Championship, television guides to tournaments and a lot of specialized pulishing activities. We do video production for the USGA, the R & A, the Masters, documentary film production things of that kind – I suppose that would be it.

'The image of my company? I think it varies. There are people who think, "Oh, my god, they do too much." Or they shouldn't be doing this and that. I would like to think that IMG is a company that does what it says it is going to do, and does it efficiently. I don't think anyone can point to anything we have done that is bad for the sport. And I think that is the criteria.

'People say they are too pervasive in too many ways and they shouldn't have so much influence. And yet nobody can point to any instance where that influence or that pervasiveness has worked to the detriment of the sport of golf. They don't do that . . . they just get resentful. I find a lot of the media in the world, particularly in Britain and maybe in Australia, don't seem to like success. They like to chip at it, pick at it. We try not to let it bother us too much. In making a positive image for our company, we try to perform well, execute our tournaments well, manage our clients well, negotiate good contracts, deliver what we say we are going to deliver and let the record speak for itself.

'The game of golf seems to work pretty well. The USGA and the R & A are together now on the rules and the equipment and so on. There is an American expression which says "If it's not broke, don't fix it." The game works. However, I think the professional tours are too provincial, too self-serving.

'You take Deane Beman in America, the commissioner who has done a remarkable job for the American tour. He has not done a remarkable job for golf. But he is being paid by the American tour, he is not being paid by golf, so you can't fault him for that. His constituents don't much care about what he does for the sport, unless it gets so bad that it's going to hurt the way they earn their living.

'People say there are no charismatic players in America any more. Anyone watching the PGA Championship might have thought we had a charismatic champion in young John Daly, who got everyone excited. I am not sure his golf is good enough. But the mental approach of the American professional has become defensive. It has been too much aimed at making a good living, getting a good cheque, getting a top ten finish. If you ask an American professional, "How did you do last week at Greensboro?" He'll say "I finished sixth," as if that's good. Or, "I got a good cheque." Ask Nicklaus or Ballesteros the same question and they'd say, "I lost." Life has become so comfortable for these people.'

Deane Beman disagrees:

'I don't accept that as a premise. It is much more difficult to win the number of events that a Jack Nicklaus and an Arnold Palmer won and a Ben Hogan won, because there are more good players. There's more competition, but that doesn't mean the public interest is any less. As a matter of fact the public interest is a great deal more. When no one could doubt today the charisma and the interest publicity-wise of a Jack Nicklaus and an Arnold Palmer, or certainly a Ben Hogan or a Sam Snead. But I can tell you today there are more people watching golf. There are more galleries. There are actual fans out there watching the Payne Stewarts, the Greg Normans, the Paul Azingers, and Curtis Strange and Tom Kites in their own way, than there were Jack Nicklaus, Arnold Palmer, Ben Hogan, Sam Snead, or Bobby Jones. So we must be doing something right.'

But that is not the only problem that Mark McCommack sees:

'Having said all that, you have all these tours around the world – four of them. And I think the American tour could vary its formats. Although the Ryder Cup ratings in the US were horrible, it was very exciting for golfers to watch, on both sides of the Atlantic, because it showed best ball golf, better ball golf, alternate shot golf or foursomes golf, and singles match play competition which we don't get a chance to see.

'People are bored with 72 holes medal play formats every week. We need varied formats. We need to make it easier for the Europeans to play in America, and for Americans to play in Europe. We need for everyone to be less territorial. There are problems with that. It is a one man one vote situation, you know, and you have 20 super stars on top, then 200 other people of whom the bottom 100 are struggling to make a living. The last thing they need is for 40 Europeans to come storming in taking money out of their pockets. But it is bad for the sport.

'And it is tragic that the Japanese don't play outside Japan more often. It is a country that loves golf, and has a lot of economic power to put into the sport, but that power is linked to their players. With the exception of Aoki and Nakajima and a couple of others over the past 10 or 15 years, they just don't play internationally.'

McCormack is by far the biggest of the entrepreneurs that the game's administrators have to deal with. Almost every area of the game which they themselves do not directly control, IMG has a say in, if not a controlling interest. But stars as clients were the foundation of his business and they remains the core operation.

The most persistent criticism that has been levelled at IMG over the years is that they rush their clients from pillar to post in pursuit of the almighty dollar, and often to the detriment of their game.

'There are lots of misconceptions, particularly about how we "make" clients do this or that, go here or there. People who accuse us of that don't know golfers. We don't make our clients do anything. We say for example to Nick Faldo that he has the opportunity to go to Japan for X dollars the week before the US Masters. Certainly it is incumbent on us to make him aware of that opportunity. He will say, "That's very nice, but I want to practise for the Masters and I don't want to make that trip before the Masters." We give him lots of opportunities of that kind during a year and he says yes or no to them. We can't make him do anything. We give them opportunities, they choose certain things. People used to say that in tennis we got Bjorn Borg to play in Germany. Anyone who knows Bjorn Borg knows he is a stubborn guy and he's going to play where he wants to play. We can tell him what we think are the pros and cons of playing in Germany, but he's going to take that ultimate decision.

'Every time any of our golfers hits a slump, it's our fault. Everyone said Ian Woosnam was playing well and IMG made him sign with another golf club company, and they've screwed up his career. Then Woosnam had the best year of his life with these clubs, became world number one. But nobody ever talks about our clients who are top of the world lists.'

Tony Jacklin, for one, would never deny this was true, but he felt that he also needed sound advice as to which of the options would be in his best interests, and this was not forthcoming: 'They assume that you can say no, but you know the carrot is there, that there's ten grand or whatever the number is, if you go and do this. And if you do it could lead on to something else. The carrot was always big and they were getting 20 per cent.'

Nicklaus must be the biggest name that ever left McCormack. But when they did part it was without animosity. As you would expect with Nicklaus it was just a sound commercial decision:

'Mark represented me in his early years and basically with Arnold and Gary and we did a lot of 'big three' television matches, a lot of exhibitions together, a lot of travelling together and we became the Big Three. Mark was handling all three of us and it was very successful for him and for us.

'IMG were the only game in town at that particular time. They handled all my stuff and were very expensive. But it was the name of the game because there wasn't any other game in town. But I didn't have any complaints with Mark because of that.

'But towards the latter part of the '60s I realized that I was always going to play second fiddle or third fiddle, whichever it might be, to Arnold and Gary. And then I didn't want to be second fiddle and I wanted really to control my own destiny and my own affairs a little more. So I started out on my own.'

For all that McCormack has retained far more clients than he has lost, the prime reason being that he has always known, better than any, the true worth of star quality and how best to place that talent in the market place.

'Maximizing the potential of a major championship winner depends entirely on who the player is. For example Jack Nicklaus winning a major today would have very little value. He's already the best player who ever lived. If a player is young, and has done nothing, but is perceived by the experts in the game to be someone with a great future, it could have great value. If a player is at the end of his career, everybody is going to think that it is very nice, but not worth much to him. If a youngster, Billy Andrade for example, were to win the British Open. . . .

'The other thing I once told Clifford Roberts at Augusta, and he wrote about it in an article later, is that the Masters in many ways is worth more than the others for a couple of reasons people don't think about. One is that most golf equipment companies launch their lines for a spring season, which means the goods have to be into the trade in the autumn. If you win at Augusta in

Jack Nicklaus went his own way.

April, you have that much more time to get a line of goods set for the autumn. The other reason the Masters is valuable is that there are two and a half months between it and the next major championship, the US Open. That gives the player's management time to get to work for him. If he wins the US Open, there is the British Open coming up three weeks later. Then three weeks after that, there is the PGA.

'This became very clear to me when Arnold Palmer won the Masters four times. He made my career. Without Arnold Palmer – if he hadn't had the confidence in me at an early age – I'd have been practising law in Cleveland, Ohio, I'm sure. He gave me a chance to demonstrate what I could do, and I feel I delivered for him, so that was good. But I owe everything I've got in life to Arnold Palmer. And I think we did a lot of things in terms of developing the Palmer brand of products. The traditional way of doing it was to have a guy endorse somebody else's product. We got people to put out Arnold Palmer clothing, like Lacoste did, to try to build a brand that would outlive the man's career on the golf course. He hasn't won a regular tour event in 20 years, yet his products are selling, I mean millions and millions and millions of dollars worldwide with Palmer's name on them. We did that pretty well, I'd say.'

On the back of his achievements with Palmer, it's not surprising he was able to sign up many of the best players around the world. But with winners of major championships now coming from all parts of the globe, it is no longer possible for one organization, however large and successful, to represent all would-be champions. Also, with so much money now available to be won on the playing fields of the game, it is now not vital to go for the most lucrative endorsement deal, especially if it requires considerable time and effort to service it.

The Spaniards Ballesteros and Olazabal are two who have chosen to resist the overtures of IMG and have gone their own route, selecting managers who look after their interests to the exclusion of all else. Joe Collett has handled Seve's affairs for several years, and Sergio Gomez is perhaps more of a guardian angel or Dutch uncle to Olazabal, rather than a win-at-all-costs super deal maker. Says Gomez, 'It's maybe because of that feeling of fierce independence the Spanish have.'

Gomez was a member of Olazabal's club, and was in charge of the youth section. He started to handle Jose Maria's correspondence and continued doing the job for fun in his first two years as a professional. Four years ago he became his manager.

'It is not very difficult. He is a very nice guy, very gentle and the only thing he really wants is to be involved playing golf. I have to take care of all other matters. He was very young when he started, you know. He knows that there is someone taking care of him only and that's perhaps what you cannot have from a big company. The game is very tough – when you play well, you say it should have been better. When you play badly it is very disappointing. And being away from home and travelling is a problem. That's why we don't have many endorsements. We have clothing, clubs, and one insurance company. They create obligations. You can be away from home for 30 weeks at tournaments. If you have 20 endorsements, that takes another 40

Senor Gomez (far right), Jose Maria Olazabal's Colonel Parker.

days. His goal is to be number one in the world. If he gets that spot, money and business will come later.'

Peter Alliss has mixed feelings on the position of managers, or agents, but tends to favour the sort of one-to-one relationship that Olazabal has with Gomez. Speaking about managers generally and the position of IMG regarding the players that they manage he says:

'I, in my naive way, thought that a true blue manager would have one client rather like Colonel Parker and Elvis Presley. You've got Elvis, you don't want any more clients. . . .

'Colonel Parker was a very lucky man to have Elvis Presley

and I think if I had been Mark McCormack, I might have stopped with Arnold Palmer.'

McCormack would reply that all his truly big name clients have their own manager anyway, with each one being allocated a senior vice president, specifically to look after their interests. In addition, they can offer a world-wide service only available through association with a substantial corporation.

Hughes Norton is IMG's man responsible for Greg Norman, the Australian golfer who is one of the outstanding personalities in golf, and a huge earner. He describes some of his responsibilities.

'It's a combination of a lot of elements. It is searching out endorsements for Greg around the world. It is organizing his schedule on an annual basis. With a player like Greg, who likes to play as much as he does around the world, that can become reasonably complicated. (He likes to go to Australia at least twice a year, sometimes three times.) He played for five seasons on the European Tour and still considers that home, in a kind of secondary way, even if he lives in Florida now. He likes to go back and play there two or three times.

'He will play a full complement of 10 or 20 events on the US Tour, so that's an organizational challenge in itself: deciding where he is going to play; the number of tournaments – always trying to balance with him the right number of tournaments to play to prepare for the ultimate goal. That is for Greg Norman, as for Nick Faldo or Ian Woosnam or Curtis Strange, whoever you name among the élite of golf, the major championship. That is what they are all focusing on. Many people think the schedule is built around income. That is only partially true – we live in a commercial world – but it is really finding the right mix. What should he being doing just prior to these major championships, so that he can be perfectly prepared for them?

'The commercial side of things is organizing contractual activities in balance with his game. That comes first. Everything flows from his golf game. If he is not playing at the top of his ability, everything else suffers. You can go to extremes in this business. You can have 40 contracts and make $40 million a year, but you are not guaranteed to play well. Greg's earnings are substantial, but are centred on three or four major agreements. An athlete like Greg Norman has two things to sell: his name and his time. The goal is really to surrender as little of his time and use as much of his name, so that his life isn't spent servicing contracts, lucrative as they may be. We made some changes in 1991, a fine tuning process in terms of his management, when we terminated several agreements that were up for renewal. They were encroaching on the time he'd rather have spent on playing, or practising, or being with his family in Florida.

'Everything is really his decision in the end. Greg signs off on everything he does, whether it's appearances or contracts or whatever. It's simply a matter of things he's interested in. Lexus is a good example. He loves high performance automobiles and he had a chance to endorse this new car, this luxury automobile that Toyota makes. If someone asked him to endorse beer mugs or glasses, no matter what the amount might be he might say well, thank you very much but I'm not interested. The amount of time required is always the question. It's usually in three or four month chunks where we'll make a schedule and pretty much stick to it. He sits down and says, "This is what I'd like to do" – and off we go.

'He is quite interested in golf course design but we've made a kind of strategic decision that for the next four or five years, until he is 40, he'll really concentrate on playing tournament golf, as opposed to designing golf courses because it is a very time-intensive activity. Jack Nicklaus might make ten or a dozen visits to a course site and that can take over your life if you have eight or ten or more course projects going on at the same time. There are about six or seven projects in Australia that bear Greg's name, which he got into three or four years ago, and which he visits during the construction stages, with Bob Harrison, Bart Collins and our staff in Sydney. But he'd like to cut that off for the moment. We talk about it a lot. When someone comes waving a million dollars to design a golf course, I say, "Greg, this is costing you money, costing us money, but we believe it is the right thing to do."'

'Each client feels that he has his own team of two or three people at IMG that work specifically and specially for him. That really is the answer to those people who accuse IMG of being too big.

'It has made some kind of public relations problem for the

company. We are conscious of the public image of IMG. We don't do as much professionally about it as perhaps we should, but our chairman has never really believed in it. He has always felt that the strength of our clients and our achievements speak for themselves. Of course, since the early days, when he represented Arnold and Gary and Jack, he probably felt, who needs a PR firm. Lots of voices in our company, and some of our outside corporate friends, say there is a much bigger place for PR in the firm.

'In terms of conflict of interest, our answer is always disclosure. We run a tournament, we represent several of the players, we make money organizing the tournament and taking commission from the players, from arranging a television contract – sure we make money from all of that. But if you disclose these interests to all parties in advance, and everyone going in understands what cards are on the table, we don't think there is conflict. If there isn't a tournament, there is no place for a Curtis Strange or whoever to play that week and have an income opportunity. That's how we look it.'

John Simpson is Senior International Vice President at IMG, based in London, and something of a minder and hand-holder for Nick Faldo in his scheduling and business life and career generally:

'IMG is a big team, and it's team work that keeps all the day to day hassles away from a champion like Nick. That's number one.

Overleaf:
Greg Norman and IMG – one of golf's commercial success stories.

Nick Faldo and **John Simpson** from IMG's London operation.

— 125 —

Number two is to maximize all his merchandising opportunities worldwide. And – number three that's to do all his financial work. Tax returns and the like. And advise him on investment. Ideally he can then get on with what he does best, and we get on with what we do best. I spend a lot of time with Nick. We meet quite regularly and since he is now in a worldwide situation, we can meet anywhere.

'Before a player wins a major championship, we would work short term, making contracts for two or three years. But when a player gets to be as big as Nick, we are thinking of ten to 15 years – in fact, Pringle have signed Nick until the year 2001.

'Our relationship hasn't changed, it's just that the work has become a lot bigger and a lot more complex, but nothing else has changed. Our relationship was based on trust, and that has not changed. Of course, many more people are involved in taking care of him. There are the girls who handle the day to day paper so that he knows exactly what he's going to be doing when he's working with his companies, or his schedules for tournaments. His acountancy needs to be on a worldwide basis, with all the income he is producing and making. Then there is the legal side and the tax side, both of which also have to be international, getting contracts in place, and correct. So its quite a vast back-room team, and getting bigger and bigger.'

Nick Faldo, thrice winner of the Open Championship and twice winner of the US Masters, looks at IMG, and life, from the other side of the fairway:

'Over the years it has really evolved. I've been with IMG since 1976, so progressively since then they have done more and more for me. The great thing about IMG is they would do as much for you, or as little for you, as you want. If you want to stay in control of things, or if you don't, that's fine. I don't, that's their job. John does the merchandising bit. The financial team does it's bit. They are all experts. So I go out and play golf. That's all I worry about. In some ways that annoys my wife, but you know, that's all I'm interested in. If it was me, they could do everything, right down to paying the gas bill. They take care of the headaches, they take care of everything off the golf course, and I worry about just playing golf. After I won at Augusta the first time, there was an incredible explosion in my "world recognition" factor. Then when I won the Open Championship, and when it all happened again – the good thing was that we had learned to be on top of it. But the team, the back-up team, just got bigger and bigger.

'It's very difficult to describe really what it does to your life. Imagine the telephone simply does not stop ringing. You put it down and it rings again and again and again. that's fine in an office, but not in your home.

'In the end we had to send out the word that nobody understands, and that is NO. We had to put our hands up and say NO. We stopped doing anything at the house; no more interviews, nothing. It was to be our only little area that we had private to ourselves. Anything I did was away from the house, even if it was only at the local golf club. And from then on, every time an interview was requested, we'd say was it good for me, or just good for the magazine. Then we'd decide!

'A well-known phrase that Arnold Palmer used a couple of years ago, "Do unto others as you would have them do to you", hit me. I would love to have known that when I was 20. I might have changed a few things. But you bulldozer along and it is pretty tough to have a wise head on young shoulders. But you learn lessons which you hope take you along to maturity. In my business, you have to be nice to everybody. The most difficult thing is the fact that you are really sometimes under the spotlight, the microscope, everywhere you go. Everything you do is public, you can't get away from it. This is great when you are playing well, and everything's fine and wonderful. You're waving and smiling, and such. But when things are not going so well, you've got everybody leaning on you, and they start asking slightly different questions, such as where the hell have you gone wrong? That is very tiring. You take it away with you. You go to bed and think of this and that and it just wears you out. That is the hardest part of fame or success. Sometimes you just want to be yourself, and you can't. You arrive somewhere and as soon as people see the face the whole thing becomes a big hullaballoo.

'But I am still as keen as ever, and feel I've got some more seasons, to the end of the century, to go. Who knows what my total golfing package will be. I don't. I'd obviously love it to mean half a dozen more majors. We are already planning life after tournaments. We are looking at golf architecture, and a golf academy idea.'

CHAPTER EIGHT

OF BOTH LINKS AND
TRADITION

.

The last of the Ice Age melted away from Scotland some 10 000 years ago. This is a fact that seldom troubles many of the world's golfers, but as we shall see, it started the evolution of the links on which the original game was played and which have influenced the development of all the world's golf courses. Simplifying complex geological processes, we can say that sea levels, at first raised by the melted ice, fell back to expose areas of flat land along the estuaries of

Turnberry joined the Open rota in 1977 and hosted one of the great Opens of modern times.

Forth, Clyde, Solway and Tay. Rich alluvial deposits brought down by the rivers fertilized this ground into the carse lands as we now know them. At the same time, on-shore winds carried beach sand inland to form dune systems; the lines of duneland paralleling the shore line. The highest line of dunes remained nearest the shore, as evidenced still at Turnberry. And the duneland was relieved by vegetation – grasses which were consolidated by bird-borne and wind-borne seeds – and bird droppings which created a tilth that also allowed heather, whins and broom to establish themselves.

In the sheltered areas, the valleys between the higher dunes, a hard-wearing, shallow-rooted sward of grasses that we now know as bents and fescues grew and the ground, cropped by rabbits and sheep, was stabilized. Meadow grasses developed in the carse lands and along the river banks, and marram grass bound the sand dunes.

This linksland, as it came to be known, was seldom more than a mile in depth and evolved in distinct areas of Scotland. Historically, it was common land, ground upon which the populace might disport

itself, rather like the village greens of medieval England. And indeed they were used in the same way for archery, pasturing sheep and drying clothes and the like. One of the most important charters in the history of St Andrews was that of Archbishop John Hamilton in 1552, confirming the right of the Provost and Town Council and towns-people to use the links.

There is some evidence that golf of a fashion was being played at St Andrews when the university was founded in 1413. The word 'links' dates from the first half of the fifteenth century. It would have been a primitive affair, and it is not unreasonable to suppose that the early players might have followed rabbit runs, widened by hunters across very uneven ground and through forests of whin and bracken. With usage, these runs or paths widened further until, given some imagination, they became recognizable as 'fair ways'. The golfers played no doubt to oases, or open areas perhaps made so by feeding rabbits, as golf 'greens'.

So narrow was the entire playing area at St Andrews, bounded to the east by high banks of whin and to the west by arable land, that by the middle of the nineteenth century for example, one putting green had to serve two holes. Eleven holes had run out from the start, then the same eleven had been played back, with putting priority given to the inbound players. But in 1764, some holes were amalgamated, to leave nine holes out, nine holes in, and so the 18-hole golf course was born. Other clubs had odd numbers of holes – Leith and Musselburgh had five, North Berwick seven, the early Prestwick had 12, and at one time Montrose had 25. All fell in with St Andrews

Why golf should have started in Scotland remains a simple freak of history, but the Old Course, as St Andrews came to be known, was destined to become the definitive golf course, and St Andrews, with the help of the Gentlemen Golfers of Leith, to become the 'Home of Golf'. And why not – after all, it was a market town, a university town and before the Reformation had been an important ecclesiastical town with a cathedral which was the pride of catholic Scotland.

The game, into the nineteenth century, was played over what amounted to virgin ground, through the dunes, between the banks of whin. At some point before 1800, 'greens' were created, some turfing was done around the hole and some efforts were made to make reasonable surfaces by the flagsticks. The first grass-cutting machine dates from 1830 and was not generally accepted until around 1870 – it was 1911 before the Royal and Ancient Club had a motor-mower! And not until 1846 were there separate teeing grounds – previously golfers teed the ball a few clublengths from the hole. Golfers fished the ball out of the hole with their fists, no doubt enlarging it. The Crail Club, founded in 1786 claims to have been the first club to have used metal liners in golf holes, in 1874.

There is a general assumption that the Old Course is a gift of nature untouched by hand. Not so. The hand of man has oft been laid on it. For example, Haskell's bunker, which no longer exists, was to be found at approximate driving range on the present first fairway. The sea at St Andrews is a retreating force, extending the ground between the Old Course and the beach so that other courses have been possible, the New and the Jubilee. In those early days, sand would often carry to where the present clubhouse stands.

In 1848, a new first green and a new 17th green were built and the course was widened, allowing the possibility of playing the course anticlockwise, which is the present routing, or clockwise. And for the first time on record, artificial hazards were put in place on the Old Course. On that sandy soil, cutting a new bunker, which had natural drainage, was never difficult. Widening the course left many of the existing natural hazards, such as whins and bunkers, between the two 'fairways' rather than on the outside of the course. This brought strategy into play by offering more than one route from tee to green around the hazards. These strategic options were to have a widespread effect on the course designers of the future, and meant the beginning of golf course architecture, which did not then exist as such. It has to be realized that in the early nineteenth century, all the Scottish courses apart from Glasgow (1787) and Perth (1842) were links.

In September 1858, Allan Robertson went round the Old Course in 79, the first man to break 80. He used a gutty ball, although he had resisted the coming of the ball and the passing of the feathery. Allan Robertson might be considered the first professional golfer in history. He also, in an unofficial way, 'supervised the green' at St Andrews and was responsible for the further widening of the fairways and enlarging of greens. So he can be considered the first greenkeeper. And since he created the famous 17th green, and also laid out some links holes at Carnoustie, he can be considered the very first golf architect, the first of what has become a remarkable profession.

Many of his contemporaries followed his lead. Tom Morris was perhaps the most industrious of them and designed courses all over the UK and Ireland. He left a startling legacy which includes Prest-

wick, Lahinch, Royal County Down, the New Course at St Andrews and Muirfield, where he was the first designer to plan contra-rotating loops of nine holes, to maximize the challenge of the wind.

These early course planners were little concerned with drawing boards or topographical maps. They simply walked the land. Theirs was a system of staking sites for tees and hazards, selecting natural sites for greens if they could find them and rearranging the whole thing into some kind of sequence of 18 holes which would return to the start. Courses might be laid out in a matter of days for a fee of a few guineas, plus travelling expenses.

In the final quarter of the nineteenth century, there was a golfing explosion as the game spread rapidly to England and beyond, and the demand for courses and their designers was huge. These men did almost nothing to alter the contours of the land. They relied simply on experience and instinct and the wonder was that so much of the general quality of the work done was surprisingly high. Perhaps the greatest of these early designers was the paragon, Willie Park Jr (1864–1925) of Musselburgh. His father, Willie Snr, won the first Open Championship at Prestwick in 1860 and three more; his uncle Mungo won it in 1874. Willie Jr, in turn, won the championship in 1887 and 1889 and was clearly one of the finest golfers of his day. But Willie was more. He was a club-maker, an author, a business man, a perfectionist, and one of the finest golf architects in history. He was probably the first man to give the profession a deep, objective study, reflected in his work, *The Game of Golf* published in 1896, which claimed: 'The laying out of a golf course is by no means a simple task. Great skill and judgement and a thorough acquaintance with the game are absolutely necessary to determine the best position for the respective holes and teeing grounds, and the situation of the hazards.'

Alas, the truth was that the immense demand for courses to accommodate the boom in golf in the late nineteenth century led to the production of much banal work in course design. Too often a course was knocked together with a square teeing ground, a cross bunker the width of the fairway, and a square flat green with bunkers front and back and on either side. Remnants of this basic model are still to be seen, at Royal Mid-Surrey (1892) for example. But the need at the time was for courses for the club or the community which could be built quickly and maintained cheaply, and if they had to be built on clay pastures which became sodden and flooded in winter, so be it. Tom Dunn in Britain and Tom Bendelow, a transplanted Scot in

Opposite:
Allan Robertson, one of the very first professionals.

Willie Park Jr, a winner of the Open Championship who turned to course designing and was responsible for the Old Course at Sunningdale.

America, were experts at producing simple plans for such courses. When Horace Hutchinson, the first Amateur Champion (1886) wrote in 1897, that 'the laying out of a golf course is a wonderfully easy business, needing very little special training', he was confirming much of the general attitude at the time. It was also a statement in direct contrast to the thinking of Willie Park. He laid out two gorgeous courses at Sunningdale and Huntercombe, opened at the turn of the century, to underscore his claim and reveal to the world the potential of the heath country of Surrey and Berkshire, to the south and west of London. This land was inland links.

It was land with a quick-draining, sand base, ripe with heather and rhododendrons rather than whin, and wooded with fir and pine. Park's courses had tees or greens raised or lowered in relation to fairway levels. The greens were large, contoured with gentle slopes. The man-made hazards were boldly sited. There were diagonal cross bunkers, carries over heather – movement in every fairway – and at Sunningdale an artificial pond, perhaps the first of its kind in Britain. This was heathland golf which in time would rival links golf and produce outstanding architects in John Frederick Abercromby, Harold S. Colt and Herbert Fowler. Their works were to include Coombe Hill, Worplesdon, Woking (Abercromby), Rye, St George's Hill, Sunningdale New, Swinley Forest, Wentworth, the Eden at St Andrews and scores of courses designed and remodelled in the US and Europe (Harry Colt), and at Walton Heath, Cruden Bay, and the Berkshire (Herbert Fowler).

Like Park, they were men of perception and imagination. Fowler for example claimed that since a huge majority of golfers sliced the ball, he should place his hazards in the main on the right side of the fairway. That simple and obvious thought is a basic rule for architects to this day. And in terms of greenside bunkers, he might place one short of the green on the left, and have another on the right, hard by the putting surface, to give some depth for the approach shot, and to give a heightened visual appeal to the target. Thus Park and these contemporaries brought architecture into the entire business.

Things were happening elsewhere. The earliest American clubs were recorded in the late eighteenth century in South Carolina and Georgia, but did not survive. The first proper American club, St Andrews in New York, was founded by John Reid, a Dunfermline man who initially laid out a few holes in a pasture, and by 1894, the United States Golf Association was brought into being by five clubs.

It appears that in the winter of 1890–91, a group of Long Island gentlemen of means, one of them William K. Vanderbilt, came across Willie Dunn of the famous Musselburgh family, at work constructing 18 holes of golf in Biarritz. They persuaded him to come to America and find a piece of land near Southampton, at the eastern end of Long Island, on which to build them an 18-hole golf course. Dunn went over in the spring and found a piece of scrubland and low-lying sand-hills, as close to linksland as could be. It was close by the resort, and with the help of a crew of 150 Indians from the area's Shinnecock tribe, from whom the course took its name, he had cleared 12 holes by the summer. Within a year, there were 18 holes, a prosperous club, and the first great American 'links' course, which endures to this day.

The Chicago Golf Club brings us to Charles Blair Macdonald, and eventually the second great American links, a close neighbour of Shinnecock – the National Golf Links of America. Macdonald (1856–1928) went to St Andrews as a young student, and quickly became obsessed with golf, and a friend of Old Tom Morris. On his return to Chicago, he built a small seven-hole course, later extending it to 18. Then by 1895, with the USGA formed, he completed the Chicago Golf Club move to Wheaton, outside the city, and the first full course 'in the west'.

The game was spreading like wildfire in the US. By the end of the century there were more than 900 courses, with at least one in every single US state, which then numbered 45. Few of them could compare with the great Scottish links. Many of them were built quickly and cheaply, but Macdonald went to the other extreme. Having read an article in a British golf magazine on the 'best holes' in the UK, he resolved to build a course in America incorporating copies of these famous holes. Twice he made trips to the old country to study holes on the Old Course, at Prestwick and North Berwick, and his travels took him from Machrihanish to Westward Ho! to Sandwich. His course would be a links, with 18 peerless holes, no expense spared and critically, the ground would be moulded to his requirement. 'The Ground determines the Play', that age-old dictum of the early golf course designers was, at last, at risk.

Macdonald eventually settled on 205 acres some three miles from Southampton, adjoining Shinnecock Hills in fact. After eight years of plotting and two of construction, the National opened in 1909. On both sides of the Atlantic, it was received with acclaim as a master work. But it was above all a revolution, a revolution in how a golf

Overleaf:
Shinnecock Hills, one of the classic early United States courses.

course might be shaped. Macdonald had vast amounts of soil moved around to shape his fairways and greens. He had 10 000 tons of topsoil moved in. He created a turf nursery and installed a complete watering system. Macdonald had coined the tag 'golf architect' in 1902. With the National, he justified it completely.

And within a year or two of Macdonald, another man of destiny confirmed that a new day had dawned. George Arthur Crump, a Philadelphia hotel owner, was the leader of a group of golfers who occasionally took the train to play at the Atlantic City golf club on the New Jersey shore near the ocean. Crump spotted a piece of ground adjoining the railway line which he thought might be right for golf. He and Howard Perrin, in time the first president of what became the Pine Valley Club, took some days off to tramp over this wild property. It was virgin land, with pine forest and fierce undergrowth, but on a sandy soil and with attractive movement in the ground.

Crump the visionary saw all of this as an inland links with trees, rather as Willie Park had seen Sunningdale. He found 18 friends to give him $1000 each. They thought this enough to build 18 holes. In 1912, they bought 184 acres of the land. Crump abandoned the city, sold his hotel, moved to a cabin on the site and started trekking the landscape. In 1913, he asked Henry Colt, then in America, to help him with the fairway routes. They produced a plan which was scarcely altered in construction. Beginning in 1914, Crump removed 22 000 tree stumps, then stopped counting. They built dams to make spring-fed lakes. Soil was brought in to shape fairways, greens and tees. Tracts of undergrowth were cleared. When Crump died in January of 1918 only 14 holes had been completed. But the club found the funds to finish the four holes – Crump was said to have spent $250 000 of his own money on Pine Valley – and the course and club opened in 1919. Donald Ross of Dornoch and Pinehurst, and certainly one of the greatest golf architects of them all, said simply, 'This is the finest golf course in America.'

Pine Valley runs through a forest, with each hole in splendid isolation from the others. There are two good-sized lakes in play affecting four holes. The fairways are islands in oceans of sand so that bunkering in the ordinary sense, and certainly fairway bunkering as such, is scarcely necessary. Pine Valley demands play from one quite specific target area to the next. The course was considered unique, and remains so to this day. The Old Course apart, it is probably the finest golf course in the world.

The real significance of Pine Valley and of the National Links before it, was that for the first time on such grand scales, the earth moved. No longer did the ground determine the play. Crump and Macdonald demonstrated that streams could be dammed, forests cleared and the landscape sculpted. Now the designer, or the architect would determine the ground. Now he would make the ground move for him.

The year 1900 is a watershed in golf history and in the story of the evolution of the golf course. It was the year in which the 'Haskell' ball came into use. It was the year of Harry Vardon's first American tour and his victory in the US Open at the first attempt. And it was the year when Donald Ross was installed at Pinehurst. The two decades which followed saw the emergence of exceptional designers in addition to Macdonald and Crump, whose talents and achievements on both sides of the Atlantic turned golf course designing into a profession.

Donald Ross, part of the strong Scottish element in early US golf course design.

The Haskell ball was 'invented' by Cockburn Haskell in 1898 and was in general use in the USA by 1900 – Vardon won his US Open playing a Haskell. The new ball ran further than the gutty, which after 50 years of service, was entirely superseded. Golf course yardages and carries now had to relate to the performance of the new ball.

Donald Ross, a native of Dornoch in the north of Scotland and a handy golfer, had been apprenticed to Old Tom Morris in St Andrews to learn the club-making craft before returning to his home town as the club's professional. Encouraged by a Dornoch visitor, a Professor Robert Wilson of Harvard University, he went to America and found a job at the Oakley Golf Club near Boston. In 1900 he went to Pinehurst as a winter professional, and remained there until he died in 1948. At Pinehurst, he set to work extending the existing course and designing new ones, with such aptitude that his Pinehurst No 2 course (there are now seven in and around Pinehurst village), is considered in the top half dozen in America. His endeavours, much praised, landed him in a design career which saw him work on some

600 courses in America, many of them with his Dornoch signature of slightly raised, tilted greens, surrounded by swales and dips which demanded a high order of short game skill from golfers. Many of his courses have become famous and have been used for national championships. They include Oakland Hills, Inverness, Interlachen, and Seminole in Florida, which was much admired by Ben Hogan, and Scioto in Columbus, Ohio, where Jack Nicklaus learned his golf.

Following the example of Willie Park Jr, British architects, in particular Henry Colt and Herbert Fowler, worked extensively in the United States and built handsome, enduring courses. A notable contemporary, alas, did not – John Frederick Abercromby only worked once outside the United Kingdom, building The Hague course in Holland.

These men, like Macdonald and Crump and presently Hugh Wilson, in America, did use drawing boards and plans. They did walk the sites. Herbert Fowler, in building Walton Heath through a heather-clad landscape, covered the area on horseback. They were concerned with turf maintenance. They laid out areas for tree planting, and left planting instructions. They took an altogether professional attitude to the business.

On both sides of the ocean, until the depression of the early thirties, golf course construction boomed. There seemed to be an abundance of funding available. The 'Great Triumvirate' of Harry Vardon, J.H. Taylor and James Braid, with their dominance of the Open Championship from 1894 to 1911, were enticed into design work. Vardon, Open Champion six times, was much in demand but did comparatively little, probably because of uncertain health. Taylor actually planned a nine-hole course at Heliopolis, in Cairo. With Fred Hawtree, the first of three generations of fine British architects, he was to redesign Royal Birkdale in the thirties, perhaps his most notable work. Braid was the most prolific of the three, leaving a vast body of work throughout the UK, the most famous of his courses being the Kings and Queens courses at the Gleneagles Hotel. Braid was not much one for foreign travel – he once designed a course in America from topographic maps, without crossing the ocean.

Donald Ross of course was active right up to his death in 1948, but throughout the twenties and thirties many talented architects emerged to work internationally, often combining in partnerships. Harry Colt spent the war years in America, but back in England in 1920, he took on a new young associate in Charles Hugh Alison, who

Opposite:
Pine Valley credited to George Crump, but with a strong Harold Colt input.

was destined to work in the USA, Europe, Australia, South Africa, and even Japan in the late twenties, where he introduced deep bunkering. To this day, such bunkers are known to the Japanese as 'Arisons'. Colt had also been instrumental in giving one Dr Alister Mackenzie a start in the business.

Mackenzie, a Leeds man in general medical practice, was intrigued with the work that Colt was doing on his home course at Alwoodley, and showed him some designs he had drawn for greens. He gave up the practice of medicine, opting for the outdoor life, and worked with Colt and Alison in partnership, before going alone in 1925. Many of his courses are considered among the best in the world; classics such as the West Course of Royal Melbourne, Cypress Point in California and the Augusta National course in Georgia. Also to his credit are the Golf Clube de Uruguay, and the Jockey Club at San Isidro, Buenos Aires.

The 5th hole on the West Course at **Royal Melbourne**, designed by Alister Mackenzie, and for many the best course in the world.

At one time, in the twenties, new courses were opening in the USA at a rate of 600 a year. Land values, labour costs and interest rates were all low, and there was design work aplenty. One of the first courses opened in that decade was Pebble Beach on the Monterey peninsula in California. It was immediately hailed as a truly great golf course with half a dozen holes along the cliff, hard by the Pacific Ocean. Paradoxically, like Crump at Pine Valley, Wilson at Merion, and even in a sense Macdonald at the National Links, Pebble Beach was plotted by men with no experience in the business; local men Jack Neville and Donald Grant. They were amateur golfers of California State Amateur Championship standard, nothing more. Ten years after Pebble Beach opened in 1919, Cypress Point, a Mackenzie masterpiece only a mile or so along the coast, was opened and although it had but three 'ocean' holes, it immediately challenged Pebble Beach in its majesty. Its 16th hole, a par three of 231 yards, demanding a shot that carries all the way across an ocean inlet, is breathtaking and has become probably the most photographed golf hole in the world.

To some extent because of his work at Cypress, Mackenzie was invited to work with Bobby Jones on his Augusta National course. It became Mackenzie's crowning achievement, the finest meadowland course in the country. Active at the same time, but by comparison unsung, was Stanley Thompson, who shared the Mackenzie philosophy that golf courses should be strategic rather than penal, and that they should give the golfer options in the playing of each hole.

He worked extensively all over Canada and as far beyond as Jamaica, Colombia and Brazil. Two of his courses, Banff and Jasper, are among the world's finest. Both are set in the Canadian Rockies in spectacular scenery; Banff built for the Canadian Pacific Railway, Jasper for the Canadian National. They reflect the strategic thinking of Thompson, and his rational but also artistic use of bunkering.

On these sites, Thompson had to be an earth mover. Vast amounts of top soil were moved in – Banff, extensively re-modelled by Thompson from a pre-war plan was said to be the first ever 'million dollar' golf course. But as much as he was famed as a designer, Thomson is also remembered as an encourager of talent. Many of his young assistants went on to have highly successful careers, and one of them became the most influential golf architect in the history of the game. In 1930 he became a partner. His name was Robert Trent Jones.

Alister Mackenzie and Stanley Thompson were disciples of strategic design in golf architecture, turning away from the 'penal' that

Overleaf:
The 16th at **Cypress Point**, probably the most photographed hole in golf and with good reason.

had been made manifest at some holes in Pine Valley and on almost every hole in a forbidding course near Pittsburgh, Oakmont, by such men as George Crump, and Henry Clay Fownes respectively, the latter a hard iron and steel magnate. They had held quite simply that a bad shot, should be penalized, should cost the golfer a stroke, or demand an exceptional recovery by him from an intimidating hazard. Jones, well trained by Thompson, was a strategist.

He was also addicted to the 'heroic' in design, the hole or the shot that would challenge a player's cold courage; the type of hole like the 16th at Cypress Point, perhaps the 8th at Pebble Beach, or the 13th at Augusta, where the golfer is tempted to bite off the corner of an angle over water or penal rough. Or as at the Augusta hole, decide between playing short with the second shot on the par five hole, or accepting the challenge of a second shot which demands a long carry to a green with the hazard.

Robert Trent Jones was born in England, and moved with his parents to the United States at the age of five. He had become a scratch golfer in his teens, good enough to be leading amateur in the Canadian Open Championship of 1927, which was won by Tommy Armour. Early in life, he had decided that building golf courses would be the thing for him. To that end, at Cornell University, he went for nothing but relevant subjects and studied architecture, engineering, surveying, landscaping, agronomy, hydraulics – and art. He served something of an apprenticeship in the thirties with Stanley Thompson.

In 1947, Robert Tyre Jones Jr, the 'immortal Bobby' and the overlord of the Augusta National golf course, asked him to revise some holes there. Jones took to the work enthusiastically. The tee for the 11th hole, formerly to the right of the 10th green as one approached it, was moved back to the left, into a chute in the woods. This, and the damming of a stream to give a little lake screening the left front of the green, changed a routine drive and pitch hole into a cracking par four of 455 yards. Similarly the tee at the par three 16th was moved, with the stream again dammed, this time to make a sizeable lake and the tee shot became 170 yards entirely over water, to a fiercely tilting green. Trent Jones, as he preferred to be called, had the chance to work on the second Bobby Jones course, Peachtree, near Atlanta, in virgin parkland, in 1954. The course, Trent later wrote, 'exemplified, we believe, the best principles of modern golf course architecture.' These principles became Jones's signatures.

CHAPTER NINE

THE TRENT JONES LEGACY

In America, the decade after World War Two was, as the decade after World War One, a decade of wealth and power. In Europe it was a decade of post-conflict hardship and weariness and reconstruction. But America, physically untouched by the conflict, strode on to new heights of affluence. The game of golf was not unaffected.

The jet aircraft transformed the travel and leisure ambitions of more and more of the population. Resort, hotel and property developers saw the sales merit in having a beautiful golf course as part of their vacation and real estate attractions, and if it was grandeur they wanted, Trent Jones was their man. He built all kinds of courses from public works courses to those of opulence and exclusivity. He built the most lavish of courses in deserts and on mountains, excavating hundreds of tons of soil, altering the course of rivers, digging out huge lakes – his use of water was quite startling – and he built huge greens with insidious slopes, mounds which drew the tag of 'elephant burial grounds', and monstrous bunkers. The more profligate Jones appeared to be with his client's money, the more clients flocked to his door. Many of his courses were quite magnificent. His business prospered and the landscape surrendered to Robert Trent Jones.

Construction, of course, had been revolutionized by the advances in earth-moving equipment. Now bulldozers and dumpers could do in a few months what horses and mules and human muscle power might have taken years to accomplish. Substantial advances were made in agronomy, in the use of fertilizers and insecticides and chemicals in general; automatic irrigation systems were developed and, all told, the business of greenkeeping became more sophisticated. Even more dramatic was the effect of the inexorable march of time. Donald Ross died in 1948: and by the end of the fifties James Braid, Harry Colt, his partner Alison, Stanley Thompson and Fred Hawtree were all gone. These had been early pioneers, putting artistry into the creation of golf courses, but Jones was the only one who had trained himself specifically for the work, with a precise, related education.

Robert Trent Jones grew up in Rochester, New York, within a mile of a Donald Ross course. That at least brought a consciousness of the existence of the game to the boy Jones. When I asked him who or what had got him involved, he said:

'Walter Hagen's sister. She was in the next seat to me in grade school, we were about 12 years old, and she said her brother was the pro at the country club and that would be a good place to go to make some money. "Doing what?" I asked. "Why, caddying," she said. From where I lived to the Country Club of Rochester was a trolley ride. You got off at Stop 6, then walked about two miles to the club. Most of the time, I ran there and back to the trolley stop. I caddied for George Eastman [boss of the Eastman Kodak Company] and the regular fee was 25¢. I kept praising him, saying, "Mr Eastman, you hit a great shot there," and so on and so on. I'd get a ten cent tip – that's a 40 per cent mark up!

'I had a feeling for the game, certainly. Harry Vardon and Ted Ray and these people would come to Rochester and play an exhibition with Hagen, and watching them gave me a feeling for the old play and the modern play and the clubs they were using and so on. Well, I got to be a pretty good amateur player in my teens. When I broke the course record at the Country Club of Rochester, I was able to make enough money to go to Cornell and study all the things that I felt were applicable to becoming a golf course architect. I learned to sketch and create hundreds of holes and greens. Having caddied and played, and seen the intrigue of it and the variety of shots hit and the need for them, I became interested and started sketching. My creativity, you can call it.

'Donald Ross did a course near where I lived. I learned a lot from that. It was sandy, and Ross put down rye grass to get the turf established. There was no watering, and he did get turf. So we were following pretty much what the British and Irish had done. The first golf courses in the United States were pretty crude. There weren't any good designers until Donald Ross came along, and he became good because he went to Pinehurst and created his nest of courses. In addition to that he was a good player and he learned how to construct these courses and did it

Opposite:
The founding dynasty of modern golf architecture: **Robert Trent Jones and his sons**, Robert Trent Jones Jr and Rees Lee Jones.

properly. That's why he built so many great courses – and they're still great. His Pinehurst No 2 is a masterpiece. Like Ross, I've always used linksland as a model. He was from that marvellous course at Dornoch, but he spent some time in St Andrews with Tom Morris.

'The basics of the Old Course are what we have all followed – the contours of the greens, the flow of their surfaces into and out of the fairways, and so on. I really don't think I have done anything different from these older fellows. I knew Alister Mackenzie and admired his work. I played golf with him and while he wasn't a great golfer, he was a great architect. His greens were sometimes severe, picturesque but challenging, with pin positions varied so that you never knew what to expect . . . Nothing was flat. His bunkering was artistic. When Bobby Jones was planning Augusta, American courses were all traps, probably 200, 250 traps. Jones thought this was unfair and unnecessary. He had a good philosopher and friend in Mackenzie. They had only about 18 traps there originally.

'You see, each hole should be a challenge, a thinking man's hole. When you create a trap in the fairway, do you give the golfer some alternatives? Can he carry it? Should he play short of it? Could he pass it on either side? What effect will it have on his subsequent shot? The shots to the green have to be good shots because iron play, approach play, is such an important part of the game. Trent Jones greens are supposed to be huge. They weren't all that way, but every time they were they made a lot of controversy. They were never much over 15 000 square feet. I look for variety in greens, picturesque greens, so that they have some beauty about them, I work on that very hard, all the time.

'A great golf course? What constitutes a great golf course is its requirements, its demands, in terms of the golf shot. The purpose of bunkering is to create a penalty for a missed shot. Think of St Andrews again. With the feathery ball and the gutty ball and different balls and steel shafts, they kept adding traps as the ball got longer. The purpose of a tee shot is to hit the ball where you want it to go to get the proper position to make the next shot a better shot, to the green. Simple strategy. A bunker is strategy, appearance, a penalty. Water of course is the ultimate penalty. There is no way of avoiding it. When Gene Sarazen created the sand wedge in the early thirties, he made trap shots a lot easier. They were no longer the penalty they had been. Trying to play a niblick, a nine-iron from sand, was a tough shot in the old days. Sarazen brought a new element into bunker play, into golf, and he was the man who created the necessity of using water specifically as a hazard. Gene Sarazen, I should say, is a very good friend of mine!

'The general improvement in equipment has changed golf course design. When I first started, you built a green a yard at a time. With modern equipment, it can be built much faster so it needs a different approach. Playing equipment is much improved. A golf club seems to be a piece of polished imagery. The top professionals can now say, "The shot is 132 yards six inches" – pretty specific! If I was teaching a young man to play professional golf, I'd have him play to a series of greens 100, 150, 200 yards away, under variable weather conditions, establishing what clubs to use, so that he has a feel for exactly how hard to hit it . . . a knowledge of ball distance.

'The game has gone to places we would never have considered when I started. Transportation has done it. When Ross was doing his courses – many courses all over the United States – he had to go overnight by train, so it took two or three days to do a one-day job. And when Mackenzie did these courses in Australia, why, he'd spend weeks getting there.'

Trent's two sons, Robert Trent Jones Jr ('Bobby', born 1939) and Rees Lee Jones ('Rees' born 1941), both graduated from Yale. Both became architects and partners in their father's business. As the practice grew, it was divided, Bobby setting up in Palo Alto, California, to cover the Western States and the Pacific Basin, his father and brother remaining at the eastern base in Montclair, New Jersey. Bobby, the loquacious one, discussing his father, explained the division.

'I think he enjoyed being a European, enjoyed the history of his own inheritance. Europe was closer. Besides, he couldn't go everywhere. Neither could I, and ours is a hands-on business, you simply have to go, have to be there. And he'd call me, sometimes at the last minute and say, "I'm not going, I'm going to stay home." So I went. I enjoyed it.'

Trent Jones at his most active was covering 300 000 miles per annum by air.

The domination of Robert Trent Jones cannot be underestimated as Ed Seay, the boss man at the Arnold Palmer Design Company shows: 'What position does papa hold? In my mind he holds number one. He is the patriarch of golf course architecture as far as I'm concerned. He is the reason people know there is a profession known as golf course architecture.'

There were other architects active besides the Jones dynasty, none more prominent than Dick Wilson. One of the busiest architects in the fifties and sixties, he built up an impressive portfolio of work, mainly in Florida and including Arnold Palmer's Bay Hill, near Orlando. Desmond Muirhead, born in England, was trained in architecture and horticulture and originally was a landscape planner. He partnered Gene Sarazen briefly, then later Jack Nicklaus on various projects, finally being substantially involved in the 'personal' course of Nicklaus at Muirfield Village, Ohio.

Previous page:
Bay Hill – the winter home of Arnold Palmer.

By the late sixties, George Fazio was established as a capable, serious designer of fine courses. Fazio had been a tournament golfer, able enough to tie for the US Open of 1950 which was won by Ben Hogan after a play-off with Lloyd Mangrum, and finish in the top half dozen on at least two other occasions. His courses were classic and graceful with the flavour of hickory shafts about them. He was joined by his nephew, Tom, and the partnership was consulted for the 1973 Masters tournament, and several times by the USGA for their championship courses. Tom has since been elected Golf Course Architect of the Year by his peers.

Things were happening elsewhere, of course. There was a new generation of architects in Britain and Europe. J.F. Abercromby had died in 1935, Fowler in 1941, Colt in 1951 and Sir Guy Campbell in 1960. Two outstanding achievements between the wars in Britain had been the re-modelling of Birkdale in the early thirties, and of the Ailsa course at the Turnberry Hotel in Scotland by C.K. Hutchinson, the work in each case leading to these courses becoming Open Championship venues. The Ailsa course was ravaged by World War Two, when an airfield was built over it, but an imaginative and dramatic design by Mackenzie Ross and determined backing by the hotels division of British Rail, produced a stunning replacement, which staged the Open Championship of 1977.

C.K. Hutchinson, Henry Cotton, Frank Pennink, Charles Lawrie, John Harris, and Fred Hawtree the son were active, but more often on the Continent than at home. Golf in England remained a rather élitist and therefore expensive pastime. The game was far more widespread in Scotland, and much more part of the national heritage, and with an abundance of fine, natural courses, the game was well within the financial scope of most Scots, particularly since they saw no need for lavish clubhouses and exotic facilities. Golf in Europe had been even more élitist than in England, and remained so at very aristocratic watering holes such as Le Touquet, Biarritz and Deauville. Only those with the highest sporting and social ambitions played the game, and the King of the Belgians, Don Juan of Spain and other royalty in exile embraced the game. Most of the courses had been designed by the British early in the century.

The most notable developments in England in the seventies were The Belfry (Peter Alliss and Dave Thomas) and at Woburn (C.D. Lawrie). The former, built over potato fields, was billed blatantly as an 'American-style' course on which Britain would win the Ryder Cup! It succeeded too – in 1985 a European team beat the United States there. At Woburn, the Duke's and Duchess's courses were built on the Duke of Bedford's estate, along contemporary American lines. In the Pacific basin, Peter Thomson, the great champion, and Mike Woolveridge, an Englishman who had played on the US Tour for a spell, then emigrated to Australia, formed a partnership that was active all over the area, including courses in India and Japan, where golf was to become a phenomenon.

The first Japanese golfer was probably Yasuhiko Mizutani, who was introduced to the game at Royal Blackheath when a student at the Royal Naval College at Greenwich, in 1898. Arthur Hasketh Groom, now acknowledged as the 'Father of Japanese golf' was an English tea merchant who went to Japan in 1868. As a mountain climber, he was so impressed by the beautiful scenery of Mount Rokko in Hyogo Prefecture that he built a summer cottage there. In 1901, he and three friends decided to build a course on the mountainside. They began with four holes on local village land, expanded to nine two years later, and there was Japan's very first golf course. No doubt it was not an Augusta National, but building on a mountainside was to become a Japanese routine, as we shall see.

The opening ceremony, in May 1903, was attended by the Mayor of Kobe and the British Consul. The early golfers, almost all foreign, travelled up the mountain to the course on foot, or by rickshaw. For a hefty Westerner, four carriers were required, two to pull, two to push. The course was extended to 18 holes in 1904. Arthur Groom, who sparked off the first 'Japanese Golf Boom', slipped on a stone on his way home from the golf club, and died in 1918, aged 72. A monument to his memory was built on the summit of the mountain. Such was Kobe golf course, Japan's first.

In 1913, Unzen, Japan's first public course was opened. The nine hole course still exists. Tokyo in 1914 was the first club built by and for the Japanese. It was laid out by Charles Alison, who aroused the interest of Kinya Fujita, a young banker who studied and worked in the United States. He went to Britain in 1919 to study Alison's techniques, and once back home, he organized the founding of the Kasumigaseki Country Club, and built its first course. In time he was secretary, captain, champion and chairman of the board of the club. The twenties and thirties were times of expansion in Japan, with foreign professionals and designers visiting and Japanese golfers going abroad. In 1933 for example, Tomekichi Miyamoto was the first Japanese to play in the Open Championship. In 1930, Walter Hagen, Joe Kirkwood, Wild Bill Melhorn and Bobby Cruickshank toured in Japan. Hagen reputedly designed the Koganei Club near Tokyo, reputed to be the most expensive in the country.

The military regime in the thirties put an end to golf, viewing it as an 'enemy sport'. Courses were used as training areas or for growing food. After World War Two there was another takeover by a military regime, this time the Americans who, however gradually, returned the courses to the Japanese, with the end of the occupation. The success of the Japanese players in the 1957 Canada (now World) Cup at Kasumigaseki, when Torakichi Nakamura won the individual prize and teamed with Koichi Ono to take the team prize for Japan, sparked off a huge expansion in the game. In the spring of 1957, there were 74 courses in the country. By the end of October, ten more had been built and by 1961 there were 263 golf courses in Japan. Kinya Fujita remained the most prominent designer, still at work on Kasumigaseki when he died there, in 1969, at the age of 80.

Despite the industriousness of its people and the sophistications of its culture, the wonder is that Japan has become such a major force in golf when one considers the disadvantages. There are some 1600 courses in Japan, with perhaps 200 more in the planning or construction stages. Indeed many people there are now saying that this is too much and three districts – Tokyo, Kanagawa and Tochigi – have banned further golf course construction. This is one difficulty for prospective course builders. There are others: the length of time involved in land purchase (sometimes as long as ten years, since there may be up to 400 owners of the required land, all of whom must be persuaded to sell); lack of expertise in agronomy and turf management; complicated government regulations; mountainous terrain, and quite astronomical costs – the construction of a typical Japanese course ranges in price from $22 to $100 million.

Kasumigaseki golf course where Japan won the Canada Cup in 1957.

The Koganei Country Club, only a half-hour drive from Tokyo is probably the unwitting reason for the present incredible cost of golf in Japan. Some years back, there was a rumour that the city government of Tokyo was about to buy it and use the land to build condominiums. The purchase price was to be shared by the club's 500 members, giving them about £10 000 each. So the price of a membership went soaring to more than £1 million, almost overnight. The example of Koganei had a knock-on effect on other clubs in Japan, since the cost of membership relates very much to the price of land.

Koganei in Tokyo – a major factor in escalating golf club membership costs in Japan.

Memberships can be bought when they are offered for sale by a member or in response to solicitations or advertisements. Brokers specializing in the buying and selling of golf memberships abound in a thriving market – there are an estimated 500 of them in the Kanto (Tokyo) area alone. Several journals are exclusively concerned with golf club memberships and current prices are published regularly in Japan's numerous golf periodicals. With this information so readily available, Japanese consumers have become more discerning, resulting in a reduction in the number of shady operators. There are four types of club membership.

    1. *Kabunushi* – (stock holder) whereby the holder owns stock in the club.

2. *Yotakukin* – (deposit) whereby an investor deposits money with a club over a long period of time.
3. A mixture of these first two systems.
4. *Shada jojin* – (juridical corporation) whereby the purchaser becomes an employee of the golf club.

The second category is by far the most common. More than half of all courses use this type of system. Some memberships are for weekdays only, some include Saturdays and some are for every day. A few courses offer special membership for foreigners, but most insist on Japanese nationality. Perhaps a quarter have restrictions on female memberships. At most others, women can join although the cost is higher than for men. As well as the price of membership itself, an investor must pay the broker a commission of two per cent, plus the substantial fee charged by the club for changing the name of a registered membership.

More recently, such has been the financial power of the Japanese economy, that famous players and famous architects have been imported to work on a seemingly endless stream of new projects – Jack Nicklaus, Tom Watson, Hale Irwin, Graham Marsh, Larry Nelson, Greg Norman, Berhard Langer, Johnny Miller among the players and Robert Trent Jones and his son Bobby, Desmond Muirhead and Peter Thomson among the designers. Japanese professionals, Isao Aoki and Tommy Nakajima, have also tried their hands at course design.

One 'foreign' designer who is totally intrigued by working in Japan, is David Thomas, the British Ryder Cup player who lost a play-off against Peter Thomson in the Open Championship of 1958 at Lytham St Annes, then was a desperately close second to Jack Nicklaus at Muirfield in 1966. He says,

'The big difference between working in Japan and working in the western world is in the scale to which you are asked to construct. Because of the restrictions on flat land, which is agricultural land or paddy fields and is sacrosanct, you just can't use that – they won't allow you to use that. So you have to go up into the mountains and build your golf courses. The earthworks are enormous. Whereas in Europe I might move 350, 400 thousand cubic metres of earth, I could be moving 3.5 or four million cubic metres in Japan. So the cost, obviously is affected. That's why golf becomes so expensive in Japan, but I enjoyed working there because of the enormity of the task.

'You go up into these mountains and they say, we want a golf course here, and you look and think how can I possibly build a golf course here. Then you go and look at someone else's and you say, "Mm, well, yes, it might just be possible." So you start to draw and start to take down hills or mountains and cut great valleys out of hills and you start building lakes in the sky because the Japanese engineers will say, "Well, we're going to fill this and its going to be 30 metres up there and we want a lake." So you are building lakes in the sky, and two years later, there it is.

'They are marvellous clients. Once you have their confidence, once they know that you know your business and what you are trying to achieve, then its go ahead and do it. They are very meticulous, doing absolutely what you ask for. I go out perhaps every two months, and if I ask for some alterations, a little bit higher here, a little bit lower there, when I go back it is done.

'Traditionally, Japanese golf courses were built with two greens on each hole, a winter and a summer green, which restricted design to a great extent. It is very difficult to produce two greens side by side and put in bunkers or features to separate them. You just can't do that, it makes for too wide an entrance into the thing. With better maintenance over the past ten years, the designer can now concentrate on one green, basically a Pencross green. So the Western architect, who knows how to handle these greens, has been asked more and more to design in Japan, but it hasn't taken the Japanese designers very long to find out where they were going wrong, and they're doing the same thing now. There are very good Japanese designers. The only criticism I have is that they are too formal, too regimented. Trees go in lines, absolutely straight, whereas we would tend to separate them, or break them up, or put them in little groups. Other than that, they are very good.'

'The government has established very strict rules for golf course construction. For instance, 50 per cent of the land in such new developments must be wooded, so each club needs a huge acreage of land per course. That makes it hugely expensive. And if it is hugely expensive for the golfer, he expects it to be very beautiful, with a huge elegant clubhouse, chandeliers and water-falls in the lobby, and so on. The costs are now so huge that memberships go to companies – it has become business, business, business, all the way.'

Now the Tokyo city government has built Wakasu Golf Links, a public course, on infill (reclaimed land). The first in Japan. The land was intended for industry, but there was a methane gas problem and the land was not stable enough for that, or for housing. So they decided on a golf course, a place of recreation, to last 10 or 15 years. Then, when the land has stabilized, it can be used for housing. Local government people from Osaka and Nagoya and other cities have looked at the Wakasu concept and are likely to copy it.

Proving man can move mountains: **Gotemba** golf course at Hakone in Japan.

Nevertheless, resort courses are increasingly popular. Although expensive, they have small memberships, opulent surroundings and a lush, natural environment. Many include other sports facilities so that the whole family can use the clubs. Japanese golfers can have many services – helicopters to and from the course, free buses from the nearest station, reservation services, computerized information on current membership prices, as well as transport for golf bags to and from the course. All of these services are sustained by the huge capital involved and invested in Japanese golf.

Perhaps significantly, of all the leading designers in the world, there is probably only one who has not yet worked in Japan. He is Paul

'Pete' Dye, born in Urbana, Ohio, and in his time a fine amateur golfer, winner of the Indiana State Championship in 1958. A year later, he left the insurance business after reputedly becoming one of the youngest 'life insurance millionaires' his company had known. He was involved in designing several modest mid-west courses. Then with his wife Alice, a first-class golfer, he toured the famous Scottish courses in 1963 and was staggered at what he saw. He became an advocate of the simplicities and eternal verities of the links golf course. In terms of landscaping, he has probably gone further than Trent Jones, has indulged in some kind of super-reformation in which the slopes on his greens are fiercer, there are more levels on them, his fairways march along like surf, his pot bunkers become even deeper. I asked him about great courses, and how they are quantified.

'Great Courses?

'Tradition has a lot to do with it. Even Augusta, a relatively new course, has tremendous tradition and Bobby Jones makes a major difference. A lot of the new golf courses today are commercial, in conjunction with a development or resort. The old time golf architects would come to town and would be told to go out and find an interesting, or a good piece of ground for a golf course. Today's design is not that way.

'The greatest defence for any golf course designer is to have a wind or some kind of climatic condition that causes a problem. Then the skillful player has to fight these elements and that makes a great golf course. Somebody said to me one day playing Seminole, in South Florida, "This is a very docile day, no wind at all, this is no golf course at all." I said it was different when the wind blows. He said you can't judge it that way. I said that the wind blows down here 90 per cent of the time – so you are right 90 per cent of the time ...! In the Old Country, if it is warm and there is no wind, these modern young players will do anything with the course. But that doesn't test them – that's not how these golf courses were meant to be.

'I've been in this business 30 years and they talk about the golf ball and the club and the shafts, but the biggest major change has been in golf equipment for course maintenance. In 1962 when Jack Nicklaus beat Arnold Palmer in the US Open at Oakmont, we thought these greens were exceedingly fast. They were about 8 [a measure on the Stimpmeter apparatus, developed by the

USGA to register speed on the greens against an arbitrary scale]. Now on any little old country club course, if we don't get them to $9\frac{1}{2}$-10, the members have a fit. The fairways you see here today are double cut and they pick up the grass cuttings. That never happened before. It has increased the cost of running a golf course and changes the philosophy of play tremendously.

'If you put in a bunker like in Scotland, with long grass with a few weeds in it, why they'd have a heart attack here. The different golf associations want the banks cut uniformly, they want the sand uniform, they want the fairways totally uniform, they want the greens uniform. Maybe I've been a little bit of a maverick here in trying to stop that trend, but it is not going to happen. In the old days we cut our greens to $\frac{1}{4}''$. Now our greens mowers have gadgets and blades which can cut to $\frac{1}{8}''$. Club members see the US Open being played on fast greens and go back to their club demanding that they have fast greens. I think it is a macho thing. In Japan now, fairways are being cut to $\frac{1}{4}''$.'

Dye designed Crooked Stick, the course on which the 1991 PGA Championship, won dramatically by John Daly, was held. He said,

'The members here have great pride in their golf course, because when it was built in 1964, it was a very severe test for the great players of 1964. I envisioned them in 1964 – Jack Nicklaus was the long hitter then, when 265 yards was an enormous drive. Now everyone hits that far. Jack Nicklaus is hitting 30 yards further than he did in his prime. Just ridiculous. When Crooked Stick got the 1991 PGA, back in 1985, I knew we would have to change the entire golf course even for one event, but the membership has such great pride that they don't want these boys to tear it apart. You see, the game is so great.'

Like most of the great course designers, Dye has a tremendous feeling for the traditions of the game, and has made the pilgrimage to Scotland to study the places where it all began. Old railways sleepers, used to shore up steep banks or the faces of bunkers on the old links greatly impressed him, though more for their aesthetic quality than for their practical use. Today, most Dye courses will be readily identifiable by the amount of timber on view, sometimes to the amusement of his fellow designers. Ed Seay once chided Dye that he may be the only golf course architect who could have one of his course burnt down.

The practical use of railway sleepers at **Prestwick** was adopted more for their aesthetic quality by Pete Dye.

While acknowledging Scotland's role in the evolution of course design, Americans will also pay considerable attention to their own traditions as Pete Dye explains:

'There have been times when one single course has altered our thinking. Macdonald and the National Links is one, Augusta is another. Go down to Augusta in summer and it will look like a cow pasture, all brown, burnt out and gone. Bobby Jones was very smart. He scheduled his tournament at the optimum time of year, when it's just one mammoth flower garden. That's only for a few weeks, but all of a sudden people in Arizona and Utah or somewhere are planning for petunias and azaleas, especially the developers. All that greenery and flower gardens sold houses, and they'd go to the course designer and say, "This is what I want." And if you are going to go to work for someone, you have to do pretty much what they say. If the Masters had been played on Bermuda grass in July or August, Augusta would have had an entirely different effect on golf course design.

'I think that Harry Colt was great. Everyone talks of Pine Valley, well Mr George Crump died during construction and somehow Colt got over there. You see a lot of Colt at Pine Valley –

I always thought he was one of the major designers in the world.

'In building and designing golf courses, you have to go back to Donald Ross – magnificent. But there is no way he could have built 600–700 courses. Where everyone is missing the boat in this business is the builder. Jack Nicklaus has a fine organization and some professional people with him in terms of the design work in setting up the bunkers and so on, but he would be first to say that if he has a first class builder, he will end up with a much better course. Tom Weiskopf works with Jay Morse. Ed Seay has been in the business for 25 years, working with Palmer, and when the golfer allies with someone like that it is a different story.

'You can sit down with a piece of paper and in two or three hours set out a strategy of how a golf course should be. It is pretty simple. Jack Nicklaus has a style, Arnold has a style, I have a style – we all have. But getting that thing built is a $3 bill. I've only built 60 courses in my lifetime. Some of the fine designers have 20–30 going in one year. With due respect to Jack and Arnold, who have produced wonderful courses, a lot of their courses have been associated with a commercial development.

'I've always said about Mr Trent Jones that right after the war there was an explosion of building golf courses in the USA and he was the biggest name in golf designers. He formed a team on how to design and build. And I'm sure the courses had much more complications and constraints than saying, "Just go out into the sand dunes and plant some grass and smooth it over." He built courses in Columbus, Ohio and Peducah, Kentucky and here and there. There had to be a good deal of uniformity there. They got the tag of the 'Howard Johnston of Golf,' but that was unfair. The USA needed golf courses, needed to get them built and to drain and to work sensibly with the environment. Mr Trent Jones did a marvellous job on that. We needed someone to provide the golf courses and he did that and people loved to play them. He wasn't given any five miles along the seaside in the sand dunes. He was sent to the sticks where they needed a golf course, and he filled the void.

'Now when this second explosion has come along, and without trying to demean anyone, when Mr Hyatt Hotel comes long, they don't go and find sand dunes to build their course, they want it wherever the Hyatt is, on whatever piece of ground they may have. The design is the simple end of it.

'A man called William Diddel, born in 1884 who lived to be 100, won the Indiana State Championship in 1904, and five times in all, a wonderful player and a great man. He probably desiged as many courses as Donald Ross – little inexpensive courses all over the mid-west. Out there in the cornfields you will see these modest courses with wonderful strategy. He said to me one day that some people in Cincinnati wanted a course and he was sure he could get me the job. I asked him why he wasn't doing it. He said they were going to put in an automatic irrigation system. He had fought this all his life and would not give in. But anyone staying in the business would have to give way to these trends. I told him I would fight them. But I discovered that I couldn't get a job unless I did give in. Unfortunately, courses all over are doing the same thing. In Japan if you don't put in enough waterfalls and lakes over there they'll throw you off the hill.'

Paul 'Pete' Dye is a traditionalist who clearly fights for the old ways insofar as they can still be applied in the modern age. He designed the hugely controversial Kiawah Island course, the venue of the 1991 Ryder Cup match between the USA and Europe, which went thrillingly to the last green of the last match on the last day, with the USA winning narrowly.

Kiawah Island is a course of rolling fairways, tightly trapped greens with dramatic movement in them, of deep greenside bunkers and tracts of unmanicured sand running the length of some fairways, in Pine Valley style. It has many of the characteristics of linksland golf in Scotland. The entire course covered a narrow strip of land running along the seashore, half the holes along the beach, the rest inland. Whereas a course like Troon or St Andrews is nine out, nine back, Kiawah had two loops of nine, each one ending back at base. More reminiscent of Western Gailes, perhaps. What was not linkslike was inland water hazards – and crocodiles.

The course was very much at sea level and the ground, particularly on the second nine, had been moved around extensively to create sand dunes with fairways running in the shallow valleys between them. The first nine was a little more inland in quality, with some trees and scrub among the sandy waste. Thereafter any resemblance with the old links of home ceased. The fairways were typically

Opposite:
Kiawah Island – now part of the Pete Dye legend.

American – soft and lush. Even on the few holes where the greens were at the same level as the fairways – the rest were elevated – the Scottish bump and run shot was not on. This had not stopped Dye making greens the size and shape of their Scottish ancestors, but he had taken one of the two methods of approach away. Also, perhaps because they were still very new, they were much harder and faster and were thus extremely difficult to find and hold, even from short range and with the technology and skills of the world's best players.

I still wonder about the necessity for the 'transitional areas' as they were called, those raked areas of sand separating fairways from scrub and unkempt dunes. By all means rake these areas, but I could not see the need for permitting club grounding; they should have been left as large areas of bunkering.

I was left with the impression that Dye had not taken full account of the wind down there. All too often during the match, which throughout was played in a stiffish breeze, the targets were too small and too exposed for the length of shot aimed at them. Much of this is critical, of course, but the Ocean course at Kiawah Island had much more to do with the excitement of the Ryder Cup than it has been given credit for. It posed questions that players on either side are not asked in their normal tour events from one year's end to the next. The course, as much as the occasion, frightened and exposed them, and the world was rewarded with some of the most exciting golf ever seen. Dye said:

'On a lot of British courses you can roll it up, sure. On Bermuda grass it is kind of hard to get that in the USA. The first year, they have what they call tip bark Bermuda, cut very short, and it is very firm. For the first year or so you would be able to run the ball on to the green, but as Bermuda grass gets older, this will not happen, they will have to pitch the ball on. The general philosophy of Kiawah was determined by its environment. We are in the USA, next to the Coast Commission, and they had all these salt water marshes and all the tidal marches, and it was dictated by all that quite a bit.

'It is the only golf course in my country that has three miles of ocean front and there are no developments around. From the aesthetic point of view – it is a beautiful golf course. The looks are filling in. We will find out later whether the course is any good in itself, but it certainly is pretty when you walk round, and as long as you don't have to play, it is pretty nice.'

Ed Seay, the strong right arm of Arnold Palmer in golf course architecture and construction, tells a lovely story of the course at Tralee in the west of Ireland, which they have designed.

'I was walking the centre lines with David Harmon, who was building the course, trying to decide on where we would put the tee for this par three hole,' he said. 'We were in a hail storm like you would not believe. We had on everything we owned – sweaters, jackets, parkas. I had a big stocking cap on. We had to shelter under a bank, like sheep in an old links course, for half an hour.

'Later, when we were telling a couple of the committee men, they said, "Oh, we would have played today if the course had been open. You know, an eight always beats a nine." You couldn't cut a log with all the clothes we had on, but an eight beats a nine is a marvellous concept of golf – you don't have to make a three or a four to be happy.'

Robert Trent Jones's son, Bobby, believes,
'All games are attack and defence. We, the golf architects are the defenders, the golfers are the attackers. When they invented gunpowder, they stopped using bows and arrows. And the great military people stopped building turrets from which to throw down rocks, and started using moats to keep the enemy at a distance. Well, we use water. We employ a variety of defences to make the player go round them, go through them, go over them and the more skillful players have strong opinions about all this. They like to hit the ball as far as they can hit it, and in their minds, every time, power should be its own reward. Not necessarily so. Skillful shotmaking, tactical thinking, makes the game more interesting.

'I'm the same age as Jack Nicklaus, we played a lot of junior and amateur golf as we grew up. He wasn't immortal in those days. We all thought we could beat each other any day, and we could. The thing that Nicklaus has done, and doesn't even necessarily realize it; he's designed his courses often around his high, floating shot. He got quite upset when I first mentioned this to him, after he built his Muirfield course in the seventies.

'I did much the same thing at Silverado. I'm a short player, but a good chipper and putter and I played there with Harvey Ward and John Brodie, the pro. We ended up all even and they said I was a little squirt who had built the course around my own game, I couldn't hit it out of my shadow but I had chipped and putted them to death.

'Nicklaus on the other hand has built courses for his long, lofted shots. At Muirfield Village in Ohio, where he has his tournament, where a Ryder Cup match is played, he has plateau landing areas down the fairways. His drive would hit the down-slope and roll another 50 yards.

'Seve Ballesteros hits it everywhere, so I guess you would design courses with a few parking lots to play on. I don't think Seve likes water as much, in some cases, because he's wilder, and the penalty for water is strong, especially in medal play, which brings up another interesting point. Most golfers, except the pros, play match play. We play for a drink or a golf ball or whatever. We have a small bet. We're playing match play because if we have a ten, we don't want the game to end there.

'The pros are playing medal play so they influence the design of a course by asking us not to create penalties which are destructive of medal play rounds. They are always trying to bring clarity to a round, they want to see everything. They want to measure everything because one stroke to them might mean $10–15 000, or even more when they are in the lead. So they always try to make the course very rational, very logical.

'Myself, I prefer to play, and many of us do, the old courses like Sunningdale or Cypress Point or Pine Valley because you can have a ten and it's not because you're looking for a ten, you might just have one, but the next hole you might have a birdie and you're still even in the match. So I think we golf architects, as opposed to the professional golfers who design courses, have to have in mind the great number of players who play the game for fun and not for money.

'A true professional architect will listen carefully to his client, study the land, and then ask the client, "Who is this course really for? Do you want to build a course for an Open Championship? If that is your idea, we can do it." We did that at Poppy Hills, where it was intended to be a course to sit among the brothers and sisters in great golfing venues, great golfing territory and terrain, and we made it a hard course purposefully, for a golf association, for their own championships. But at a place like

Wisley, in Surrey, the most important championship will be the club championship. There is no intention to have a professional championship there. They might have an event of some kind but it isn't intended to compete with Wentworth. You can't be all things to all people. There should be championship venues.'

David Thomas has said,

'I like to think that I am producing a golf course that people will enjoy. That is the prime objective. I like to hear people coming in from a round of golf and saying "I did enjoy that." I was at Sunningdale for five years as the playing professional, in the sixties, and Sunningdale I think is probably the most pleasant golf course to play on a daily basis in the entire world. You come in from a round of golf at Sunningdale and you're always ready to play another nine holes. And I think that, to me, is the ulti-mate. If I can produce golf courses that make people say, "Oh, come on, let's go and play a few more holes," I shall be very happy.'

Lee Trevino is one of the most incisive thinkers in the game. He has his own philosophy:

'I build the type of course that's playable by juniors, ladies, seniors, high handicappers. I don't even want a golf pro on my golf course. A golf pro first of all wants a free cart, wants an immediate tee time, and he's not going to pay a green fee, right? So why do I want him on my golf course? I don't want a golf tournament on my golf course – it costs you money.

'These architects build courses for publicity, but they build courses that the general public can't play. They've got courses at these resorts that would go bust in Kansas City or Chicago or LA, but if you put them with a hotel, they make it. Why? Because when people go on vacation they leave their brains at home and take their credit card. When they go a hotel they don't care what it will cost. "There's a golf course honey, I'm tired of the beach, I'm tired of this, tired of that, we'll rent some clubs, come on, let's go!" You put these courses in cities, where you have to depend on memberships, and they won't make it. People just can't play these courses. I live for the day when I can get the job to re-do one of these courses. It's not going to be very hard, all I'm going to do is get one 'dozer and push all of those silly mounds into the pits they've put there, and level the thing out, that's all.'

CHAPTER TEN

REGARDLESS OF EXPENSE

.

David Thomas says, rather wistfully,

'I think the traditional architecture of Mackenzie, Colt and these fellows was straightforward and natural, and the best. They seem to have had the best sites – Sunningdales and Wentworths, You don't find sites like that any more. Now we are given two football fields and asked to produce a Royal St George's. In actual earth-works, these fellows had very little to do. They were lucky. They followed the landscape. Now, apart from the purchase of the land in the first place, the greatest single cost in golf course con-struction is the earthwork.'

The idea of a committee forming a golf club for the sake of playing the game and nothing else, has faded. Where it has happened, it has required the sale of membership fees or shares or bonds running into many thousands of pounds in the UK and huge sums in Europe and the USA. The situation in Japan scarcely bears thinking about.

In the fifties and sixties in the USA there was a realization that in having a home on a golf course, you were living in a beautiful environ-ment, and in particular, if you had a fairway site, someone else was cutting your grass! So real estate began to dominate the economics of golf courses. In the resort hotel business golf, even back in the twen-ties, had been seen, in Florida certainly, as a prime business asset.

In the seventies, there was something of a revulsion when pro-moters over-developed and saturated their estates with housing to the detriment of the game. In addition, environmental issues often required large parts of the land to be left untouched. The Mauna Kai resort in Hawaii with its Robert Trent Jones course, reserved great tracts of land specifically for golf. Trent Jones built – designed and constructed – the entire Spyglass Hill course at Monterey in California for less than $500 000 in the mid-sixties. That is less than half of Jack Nicklaus's design fee today.

The potential promoter, developer or owner of a golf course must have a clear list of priorities and objectives. The first requirements are bravery and patience – he will be running barefoot through burning cinders for many months. He must buy the land, with some certainty that he will be allowed to build a golf course on it, and that the ground is suitable for golf. This means negotiating and agreeing with the existing owner, and having the approval of the local government authorities and other relevant public bodies with regard to planning permissions. If it is to be a real-estate venture, with permanent housing, it had better have reasonable highway and/or rail access from a metropolitan area. If it is to have holiday homes, or second homes, then it might be more remote.

One of the success stories in the business is that of St Mellion, near Plymouth in the southwest of England. It is owned by the Bond brothers, local farmers who were inclined to let the world think that they were no more than just good ol' country boys, but who have created a marvellous development which includes the first Jack Nicklaus course in England. The brothers were very successful farmers who concluded in the seventies that there was going to be a huge future in top market leisure. They built a hotel and a golf course, wanted another course and thought Nicklaus was the best in the world. Herman Bond said,

'When we went to America, Jack had done an itinerary for us. We jumped on twelve planes in six days, and that made up my mind. I think Jack wanted to work in England. We brought him over, showed him the site. We thought we had ample acreage but he said we had to purchase more land. I don't think he would have done it if we had not bought the extra land.

'I think Nicklaus is the cream of golf, one of the nicest business men I have ever met, and he certainly helped us a long, long way. We started with one golf course, now we have three and we may build another. We have an international tournament on the European Tour, and we think St Mellion has a huge future in this part of England. We were fairly good farmers, or lucky farmers; we robbed our farms to build this course, we worked hard. The course cost us about £4 million, but the bank was behind us, we never had financial problems, and it went on from there.'

Above:
St Mellion in Cornwall –
the first course by
Nicklaus in Britain.

Opposite:
The 17th on the TPC
course at **Sawgrass**, one
of the early stadium
courses, a concept
pioneered by Beman and
the US Tour.

The Bonds had followed a golden rule in these matters – hire the best experienced professional advice you can, as early as you can. And despite owning the land – they still farm some 1500 acres – the costs of St Mellion seem high even by US standards. Or perhaps they are just Jack Nicklaus high.

Ed Seay worked for seven years with Ellis Maples, whom he considered to be the best architect that ever lived. Maples had worked with Donald Ross at Pinehurst for eleven years. Seay now works with Arnold Palmer, heading up the Palmer Course Design Company. He is inclined to dub himself a 'Florida redneck', but he is certainly loquacious on the subject of feasibility reports.

'I have been in this work for 27 years, and I have never seen a negative feasibility study, never. Every one says we have the perfect piece of land, we'll sell 7000 units and make a million dollars. They come up with these financial buzz words, a piece of paper saying they'll sell 350 units at a quarter of a million

dollars each in one calendar year, and we'll spend so-and-so on infrastructure, and in five years we'll put $80 million in profit in our pocket. They take that to a bank or lending agency and they say, that's cool, you'll be able to pay back our $25 million loan easy! Now why would anyone start a $25 million project with only $6 million in the bank? I spend half my time talking ourselves out of work by telling these people that if they borrow $20 million, three years from now they have no sales, no project, and still owe the money.

'My daddy used to call it the "cigar box theory" – if it ain't in the box, you don't go get it. Arnold Palmer is very conservative with money – other people's money. I say to these developers, "Keep a couple of million back. What happens if we get storms and winds like we had last week? How many days has it rained? If you've seeded your course in a clay condition, you don't have any grass – it's gone. You'd better have that $2 million in the sack, somewhere."

'On the cost of golf courses, we have a general rule of thumb, expressed by our computers for geographical areas of the country. The northeast, the mideast, the midwest, the west and so forth – Hawaii, well that's wild. Unless you have very severe ground, or something exceptional, it's about $200 000 a hole, somewhere between $3.5 and 4 million. We've just built one at Gulf Shore in Alabama for $2 million, but that was on a turf farm, a gorgeous piece of ground. Our fees would run anywhere from 10 per cent to 20–25 per cent of the total cost. The name "Arnold Palmer" means a lot. We have letters in the files which prove it. We have one from the guy who says he can sell his lots for $19 000, but with Arnold Palmer's name on them, for $68 000. What do you care about a fee if you want to have Arnold Palmer. What do you care about fees if you want Vladimir Horowitz to play the piano for you, or Zubin Mehta comes to conduct your band?'

An inspired concept of funding for golf courses has been created by Deane Beman and the PGA Tour. PGA Tour Investments Inc., is charged with being co-promoter, co-investor in the first place, of a series of golf clubs throughout the country entitled 'The Tournament Players' Club'. The first one was opened in 1980 and by 1992 the total had passed 17, with one opened in, to no one's surprise, Japan. Vernon

Kelly is the director, and an expert on the financing of golf courses.

'The most common funding in the United States is in association with real estate development. Developers traditionally have built large, mixed-use projects, and they have to have a golf course to be competitive. The course is simply an amenity that assists real estate sales. Our TPC courses are slightly more expensive than a normal developer's course because they take a little more acreage to accommodate our tournament functions: the gallery, TV pad, parking and hospitality, that kind of thing. In addition there are costs involved in electronic wiring and the like.

'Generally, a good golf course can be built for about $4 million; three and a half to four million for the course itself. In addition to that, the clubhouse might well cost the same. Then there are soft costs for design fees, surveying, engineering, overhead construction management, then furniture, fixtures and equipment. That list will include golf carts, golf course maintenance machinery and equipment, fixtures in the clubhouse, kitchen equipment, that type of thing. So I would say about $10 million at the low end, $15 million for a really first class facility. And all that assumes that it is built on an average site.

'With a Tournament Players' Club the development would run probably to a minimum of 800 acres for an 18-hole golf course, of which 200 acres would be for the course, 600 developable. For a 36-hole golf operation, it would be 1500 acres and upwards. The overall total development may be into the hundreds of millions of dollars so that the golf cost is not a major cost. Unfortunately it's a cost that occurs at the very beginning and has to be funded and carried until the real estate sales bring in revenue, or the cost comes back in through membership sales, or whatever.

'The value to a developer in associating with the PGA Tour occurs at a couple of levels. On one, the PGA Tour is probably the ultimate name in golf in terms of establishing credibility for the golf course. We can show a successful operation which has been in business for ten years. People know that our courses are maintained at the highest possible level, and they know that when they arrive to play golf, they are treated with the highest consideration.

'In addition to that of course, the major factor is the fact that the course stages a major PGA Tour event. If it is televised, the course and the development get national recognition and promotion. If it is not a televised event, nevertheless the event itself is a major happening within the community. And real estate is frankly a local market. Thus it is a major marketing tool. If the golf course is associated with a hotel, a televised event is clearly a major advantage. The hotel will be hoping to attract guests from all over the country, and when they see the course on television, they know that they can go there and play in the same arena as the superstars.'

PGA Developments and Beman conceived the idea of stadium courses covered with built-in mounding round fairways and greens specifically for spectators. In places guaranteed to have large crowds, such as at the 18th green and the 1st tee permanent steps have been built into the mounds.

'Stadium golf is really a misnomer – it conjures up images of bleachers. Sawgrass is about the extreme as stadium golf goes. The bulkheaded, tiered sections accommodate a lot of people for viewing the first tee. The spectator mounds are really small hills which we believe blend into the golf environment, isolating a hole and protecting it from development and also allowing people to view play. They look down on the golf with an uninterrupted view. All in all the concept has been successful from the first day this course hosted a tournament.

'Traditionally when a development goes wrong, and we've been fortunate to avoid most of these, the developer will be under-financed or have underestimated his financial requirements. (The real estate market has been extremely weak these past couple of years.) He will have based his revenue stream on an unrealistic pace of sales and ends up not having the cash flow to finance his debt. We have tried first to associate ourselves with absolutely premier developers who have the staying power to go through a real estate cycle. And secondly, we operate on very, very conservative assumptions, knowing that in the worst case our projects will probably be able to attain the projected pace of sales. Once the project is up and running, the cost of operations should be covered by dues.'

One of the ironies of this strange game is that Europe's Florida – the Costa del Sol along the southern coasts of Spain, has experienced all the mistakes that have been made in golf developments in the United States, another classic example of developers failing to do their homework. David Thomas explained:

'The commercial logic behind the building of golf courses on the Costa del Sol was the sun, winter sun. In the late fifties, in preparing for the coming season, I would go down to the South of France during the winter. Southern Spain and golf didn't exist then. The development of the urbanization and the golf course encouraged people to come to Spain, either as second home owners, in retirement, or as tourists. Unfortunately, many developments have gone sour because of greed, the greed of the developer who decided, as long as he had a golf course, his properties would sell. Unfortunately, he wasn't aware that he had to build a proper golf course. Too often they were what we call Mickey Mouse golf courses. A lot of unsuspecting people bought property off the plane, from the brochure. Promised a private, championship course, they bought. Then they found the finished product was a long way from that. So began buyer resistance, when people began to say "Let me see the finished course, then I'll buy." So a lot of promoters and developers had their fingers burned.

'On top of that, many surviving courses have charged ridiculous green fees by European holiday standards, and the image of Spanish golf, of Costa del Sol golf, has gone right down. People now find that they can have a week's golf in Florida, including flight, more cheaply than they can on the Costa. Over the past ten years, so many golf projects have been started here and have been hopelessly under-funded. Developers depending on sales in a time of recession, could not hope to succeed. In any case they failed because it shouldn't be that easy to make a lot of money, it should be difficult.

'At San Roque, for example, we have an investment that is probably in the region of $35–40 million so far with, in a sense, very little return. The finance behind San Roque is Japanese, a Japanese company which in Japan owns and operates ten golf courses. They wanted to expand internationally and asked me if I had a project or knew of a project in which they could invest. I brought them to the coast, we looked at several pieces of land, and eventually a wonderful piece of land was found and within

30 minutes, they decided that was what they wanted. There was a client who had the resources to sit back and wait, and look at the long term, not the short term. With that capability, I think you will always succeed. It's the short term that makes for disaster. Underfunded, looking for membership fees to let them do the next stage – that's disaster.

'At San Roque, it's simply a case of continuous development. After four years, we are still a long way from being finished. It's only now coming together. Over the next two or three years, and with a European Tournament Players Championship scheduled, we will have a success story at San Roque – basically because the

proprietor is prepared to sit and wait for it to happen. We now have a 100-bedroom hotel which will generate cash flow throughout the year. We have about 100 fairway plots, very expensive. Then there are apartments, condominiums, and townhouses to be built at two locations – one at the top, one at the bottom of the property – with about 220 units on each site. So the generation of capital in the future is enormous. The initial investment will be returned, two-fold, I would expect. Trying to sell everything in the first year never works. Peter Alliss and I opened Sotogrande, the first Trent Jones course in Europe in 1965 – and they're still building houses at Sotogrande today!'

San Roque: a development intent on not making the same mistakes as some earlier Spanish projects.

CHAPTER ELEVEN

WHERE TO NOW?

.

Golf has travelled a long way during the twentieth century and can look back with a good deal of satisfaction on what has gone before and where it now stands. Its champions have universally enhanced its reputation and most would acknowledge that the game itself demands so much in the way of character and self discipline that only those with all the right qualities and instincts can achieve greatness at it.

Golf has survived pretty well its inevitable association with the commercial world and that in itself is a tribute to the strength of the administration of the game, which was in place well before big business turned to sport as a means of displaying its wares. Following their example, the various bodies that have emerged to run the professional game have done so with commendable integrity.

But, most importantly, golf has handled the massive explosion in the numbers that play it in such a way that its mores and customs remain in tact. To the aficionados, the game has become too slow and some of the finer points of etiquette have been trampled in the endless pursuit of the perfect swing and the desire to knock another couple of shots off our handicap.

So, what of the future? At grass roots, the game will continue to expand as fast as the creation of new courses will permit. In Britain, many courses are being built in answer to the R & A's identification of the need for some 700 new courses by the year 2000. After a silly season, when every new course was to be a championship one, with enormous joining fees and subscriptions, more practical developments are now taking place, which will meet the demand for golf facilities at a price that most can afford.

Continental Europe is the last part of the capitalist world to embrace golf as a mass participation sport and over the next 20 or 30 years a dramatic expansion of the game there is likely. Not far behind, probably, will be the liberated countries of the old Soviet bloc. Once they realize that pleasurable pursuits are no longer a crime and have raised their standard of living, they too may well embrace the game of golf.

In America, the stated need is for a new course every day till the end of the millenium. This will add just another couple of million players to the 25 million that play there now. Japan is bursting at the seams, and with their economic miracle at an end, so too is their ability to buy up the best course in other countries. For the time being, the millions of Japanese whose only golfing pleasures are to be found at the driving range, will have to stay with their noses pressed up against golf's window pane.

The 1980s saw, with the emergence of Europe and a batch of world class golfers from Australia, a shift in the game's balance of power. The total domination of the United States is probably at an end, though with three of the four major titles within their boundaries, they will continue to be the strongest single nation.

The major championships will remain the yardstick by which the best players are measured. Unfairly, run of the mill US tour players fill the bulk of the spots in the three majors played in America; only the cream of other world tours get access and their current measly allocation is only after many years of lobbying for fairer representation. Ken Schofield has been at the forefront of that effort.

'We must hope that Europe and the rest of the world can gain more access to the three US majors as we see them. We must continue to show our friends over there that the European Tour is going forward, is producing players who are very competitive and with the four majors, the public in all countries want to be assured that the best players are there. We frankly feel that this stretches to more than five or six of our Tour.'

There will continue to be much debate as to whether the structure of the major championships will remain constant. Can the US PGA hang on as a major, coming as it does so close behind the Opens of America and Britain, and without any traditional and identifiable feature to underpin its position? This is the championship Deane Beman must have in his sights as he does all in his power to promote his TPC tournament as the major-in-waiting:

'With so many good players out there, it could be good for golf to have more majors, rather than just a select few. If in fact there were five or six major championships to give individual players more opportunity to excel at those important events, then it may well be in the interest of golf for that to happen.'

But the traditionalists, and those who have lived with the game for most of their lives see extra majors as unlikely. Michael Bonallack, secretary of the R & A is one: 'There are four major championships, and I think there are likely to stay four major championships.' Greg Norman agrees, 'You've got your four major tournaments, just leave it at that. I think they are the best yardsticks to have.'

From an administrative point of view, little change is likely. No sporting body is held in higher esteem than the Royal & Ancient and their consultation and cooperation with the likes of the USGA, the professional tours and the PGAs ensures a generally harmonious working relationship.

The only cloud on anyone's horizon hangs over the US PGA Tour. After decades of almost uninterrupted growth, there are a couple of issues which have the potential to cause serious ructions. Most serious is the battle with the Ping Corporation over the legality or otherwise

Ian Baker Finch, part of an ever-widening band of major title holders.

of square grooves. The Tour wants to ban them on the grounds that their controlling effect on the behaviour of the golf ball reduces the need for the best players to develop their skills to the fullest. Ping sees this as illegal interference with their trade. The case with hundreds of millions of dollars hanging on the result started in November 1992 and the Tour is far from certain to win.

Then, the US Internal Revenue is looking at the tax loophole that allows companies to use charitable association as a means of taking the cost of sponsoring tournaments 'above the line'. Should this exemption be removed, it could have serious implications for the huge prize funds that the American pros currently play for. Many would see this as being no bad thing; the vast sums available for reasonably high finishes week in week out make millionaires of players after only a year or two, without requiring them ever to win a tournament.

On the business front, many wonder about, and not a few long wistfully for the day when Mark McCormack finally hangs up his commercial clubs, and ponder who within his organization will pick up the torch, and even if there is a potential successor to the boss. To this day, he still does all the important deals and personally liaises with all the major bodies of the sport. Make no mistake, when, and if, he does retire, that will be the moment when the sharks will come out to see what there is for them to feed on.

Perhaps the most interesting and important match in the immediate future will be the contest between the administrators and the manufacturers to keep technological advancement within bounds. Certainly, the vast sums that have been spent on research in recent years have caught the authorities somewhat by surprise, and their regulations have buckled in the face of new products and ideas. Michael Bonallack recognizes this and the R & A will do what has to be done to ensure the game remains 'honest':

'I think technology has to be controlled. We have the limits there to do it and we're going to concentrate more and more on these areas, because you never know what might come up with the tremendous amount of technological advances being made – materials that have been used in space projects for example ...'

David Fay, his counterpart at the USGA is of like mind:

'You want to retain the skill factor and I think we have done that through our Implements and Ball Committee. But you certainly can't put a complete harness on the technological improvements.

And the improvements are also in the condition of the players, they're taking it more seriously.'

The best players of this and past generations agree and the manufacturers are therefore a bit on the defensive over the accusations that they are ruining the game. Wally Uihlein of the Acushnet Company says there are factors other than the improvements to ball and club that have caused the dramatic improvements in the game.

'This great game has been with us for over 300 years. It has survived the Haskell, the steel shaft, the metal wood; it has survived the investment casting process and it's survived the two-piece construction ball. It has survived a lot of revolutions already and it will continue to survive, but I believe that the game will have to accept four important facts.

'One is the fundamental acknowledgment that the game of golf is a very large commercial enterprise – that we have over 40 million golfers around the world today. If you take into consideration direct spending, on both equipment and facilities, and indirect spending associated with travel and lodging, you have an industry in excess of $30 billion. That is a big business. So to go forward we must acknowledge the commercial size of golf today.

'Associated with that is that we have to insure the game stays inclusive. All of the vested interested groups, the R & A, USGA, architects, manufacturers, should meet annually to discuss in an open environment the issues and subjects of technology versus tradition. This is something that is long overdue. It is needed. It must be conducted without concern for litigation or restraint of trade accusations, and it can be done in an open, summit-type forum where everyone is allowed to express an opinion, as it represents their interest group.

'The third thing that must happen is that the ruling bodies, the R & A and USGA, must accept some representation on their executive committees by the manufacturers. They regulate equipment ... they have decided to assume the responsibility for the fate and direction of the manufacturers. This is the only way to ensure that the process remains a participation, and not a confrontation. And finally, the media in all its expressions must bring the issue of technology versus tradition constantly to the forefront. The subject is one that affects everyone. It doesn't just affect the USGA and the R & A. It doesn't just affect the manufacturers. It doesn't just affect the architects. It affects everyone who plays the game, and the great thing about this game is that it is a civil game. Disagreements have been with us for the last 140 years and they will continue. They need to be resolved in a civil manner. That is the essence of the game of golf.'

Of course, it is only at the pinacle of the game that *all* the advances can be fully utilized. It doesn't matter what grooves or ball you have, if you thin it, or fluff it, or hit it off the shank you are not going to play well. Lee Trevino, as you might expect, sums it up the best:

'Golf is doing great. Why change it? I mean, they're all arguing over square grooves and v-grooves and slick grooves and titanium shafts and graphite shafts and bamboo shafts and big grips and little grips. The human still has to hit it. Believe me when I tell you this – it's not the arrow, it's the Indian.'

Lee Trevino celebrates his victory at Shoal Creek in the 1984 US PGA Tournament and starts a trend for the over 40s in the major championships.

INDEX

Prestwick 10, 11, 13, 23, 95, 132, 134–5, 137, 166
Price, Nick 71
Professional Golfers Association *see* PGA; US PGA

Ray, Ted 27, 92, 102, 107, 150
Rees, Dai 75
Reid, John 136
Richardson, Steve 40
Rider Cup 20
Rivero, Jose 80
Roberts, Clifford 104, 120
Robertson Allan 133
Robertson, R.H. 13
Rochester Country Club 98, 150
Rodriguez, Chi Chi 66
Rogers, Bill 73
Romero, Eduardo 58
Ross, Donald 140, 141, 143, 149, 150–1, 153, 167, 168, 176
Rotella, Dr Bob 71
Royal and Ancient Club (St Andrews) 8, 9, 10, 13–14, 15, 18–19, 20, 21–2, 23, 25, 50, 75, 91, 95, 97, 116, 132–3, 168, 184, 186, 187, 188–9
Royal Birkdale Club 77, 143, 156
Royal Blackheath Club 10, 157
Royal Calcutta Club 12
Royal Liverpool Club 13, 77, 97, 99
Royal Melbourne Club 144
Royal Mid-Surrey Club 33, 38, 135

Royal St George's Club 29, 34, 98
Rubens, John 42–3
Ryder Cup 20, 30, 32, 34, 38, 45, 46, 50, 53, 66, 67, 72, 109, 117

St Andrews, New York 20, 136
St Andrews (Royal and Ancient) 8, 9, 10, 13–14, 15, 18–19, 20, 21–2, 23, 25, 50, 75, 91, 95, 97, 116, 132–3, 168, 184, 186, 187, 188–9
St Clair William 10
San Roque 181–3
Sarazen, Gene 28, 29–30, 75, 94, 98, 102, 105, 153, 156
Sawgrass Club 57, 177
Schofield, Ken 53–4, 58–9, 185
Seay, Ed 156, 165, 167, 171, 176
Seton, Sir Henry 10
Shankland, Bill 40, 42
Shinnecock Hills Club 20, 101, 137
Shute, Densmore 98
Sikes, Dan 60–1
Simpson, John 125, 128
Simpson, Scott 71
Snead, Sam 47, 60, 67, 102, 103, 117
Stewart, Payne 58–9, 91, 117
Strange, Curtis 65, 102, 109–12, 117, 123, 125
Sunesson Fanny 79, 80–1
Sunningdale 27, 36, 75, 136, 140, 172

Taylor, J.H. 25, 26–7, 34, 97, 100, 143

Thomas, David 51, 157, 161–2, 173, 174, 181–3
Thomas, Frank 84–7
Thompson, Stanley 145, 147, 148, 149
Thomson, Peter 21, 58, 98, 100, 157, 161
Tillinghast, A.W. 101
Torrance, Bob 79, 90
Toski, Bob 71
Tournament Players' Club 109, 178–9, 185
Travis, Walter 13, 82
Trevino, Lee 32, 44–5, 46–7, 53, 61, 65, 74, 77, 83, 92, 94–5, 109, 173, 188
Turnberry (Ailsa) 99, 130–1, 156
Turner, Tom 75

Uihlein, Wally 87–91, 188
United States Golf Association (USGA) 13, 14, 17, 20–1, 22, 50, 84, 90, 91, 116, 186, 188–9
US Amateur Championship 20, 54, 82, 92, 94, 108
US Masters 16, 29, 30, 46, 53, 67, 72, 78, 94, 103–9, 112, 115, 116, 120–1, 129
US Open 16, 20, 27, 29, 30, 32, 38, 40, 43, 44, 46, 52, 54, 72, 79, 82, 92, 94, 95, 98, 100–2, 103, 108, 112, 115, 121, 141, 185
US PGA 27
US PGA Championship 45, 102–3, 108, 115, 117, 121, 185

US PGA Tour 15, 16, 29, 43, 50, 54–8, 59, 60, 92, 94, 98, 178, 179–80, 186–7
US Senior Open 20
US Seniors Tour 46, 47–8, 56, 60–1, 65, 90–1

Vanderbilt, William K. 137
Vardon, Harry 25, 26, 27, 34, 92, 97, 100, 102, 107, 141, 143, 150
Vicenzo, Roberto de 77, 99
von Nida, Norman 58

Wales, George, Prince of 29, 34
Walker Cup 14, 20, 39, 54, 65, 92
Wannsee Club, Berlin 36, 37
Ward, Harvey 171–2
Watson, Tom 62, 90, 94, 99, 100, 161
Weiskopf, Tom 53, 167
Western Open 54, 55, 105
Whitcombe, Charlie 76
White, Jack 27
Wilson, Dick 156
Wilson, Hugh 143
Wilson, Prof Robert 141, 145
Woburn 157
Wood, Craig 29, 105
Woolverdige, Mike 157
Woosnam, Ian 34, 48, 58, 70, 77, 78, 79–80, 90, 102, 118–19, 123
Work, Bertram 82
Wynn, Oliver 33

Zaharias, Babe 65, 66
Zoeller, Fuzzy 112